The Churches Of Rouen

You are holding a reproduction of an original work that is in the public domain in the United States of America, and possibly other countries.You may freely copy and distribute this work as no entity (individual or corporate) has a copyright on the body of the work.This book may contain prior copyright references, and library stamps (as most of these works were scanned from library copies).These have been scanned and retained as part of the historical artifact.

This book may have occasional imperfections such as missing or blurred pages, poor pictures, errant marks, etc. that were either part of the original artifact, or were introduced by the scanning process. We believe this work is culturally important, and despite the imperfections, have elected to bring it back into print as part of our continuing commitment to the preservation of printed works worldwide. We appreciate your understanding of the imperfections in the preservation process, and hope you enjoy this valuable book.

BELL'S HANDBOOKS
TO CONTINENTAL CHURCHES

ROUEN

ROUEN CATHEDRAL FROM THE PONT CORNEILLE.

THE CHURCHES OF ROUEN

BY THE
REV. THOMAS PERKINS, M.A., F.R.A.S.
RECTOR OF TURNWORTH, DORSET

AUTHOR OF "WIMBORNE AND CHRISTCHURCH,"
"HANDBOOK TO GOTHIC ARCHITECTURE," ETC.

WITH FIFTY ILLUSTRATIONS
CHIEFLY FROM PHOTOGRAPHS BY THE AUTHOR

LONDON GEORGE BELL & SONS 1900

PREFACE.

THE descriptive chapters of this little book are the result of personal observations made during a visit to Rouen in May 1900, undertaken for the purpose of examining and photographing the chief churches of the city. While thus employed I made use of sundry guide-books, French and English, and collected all the information I could from vergers and others connected with the churches. The scaffolding which at that time covered the west front of the Cathedral rendered it impossible for me to examine this part of the church; any description, moreover, that I could have given would have been of little value in pointing out features to be studied, as many, when the scaffolding is removed on the completion of the restoration, will have been altered, if they have not entirely vanished. The west front of St. Maclou was also undergoing some repairs, and owing to the overhead wires of the tramways it is no longer possible to get a satisfactory general photographic view of St. Ouen from the N.W., so that in three cases the blocks illustrating the book have been made from photographs taken some time ago; all the rest are from my own negatives taken in 1900. I obtained much historical information from a book published in 1847, entitled *Album Rouennais*, illustrated by lithographs and written by Charles Richard, Keeper of the Municipal Archives and permanent Secretary of the Royal Academy of Rouen; also from a charming and picturesquely written book, the *Story of Rouen* in the "Mediæval Towns" series by Theodore Andrea Cook, published in 1899.

My thanks are due to Canon Barrie for permission kindly granted to photograph the interior of the Cathedral, and to M. Edouard Julien, the intelligent sacristan of St. Ouen (well known to most visitors to Rouen), who obtained for me a like permission from the Curé of his church.

T. PERKINS.

TURNWORTH,
September 1900.

CONTENTS.

	PAGE
INTRODUCTION	1

THE CATHEDRAL CHURCH OF NOTRE DAME.

	PAGE
CHAPTER I.—HISTORY OF THE BUILDING	7
CHAPTER II.—THE EXTERIOR	21
Portail aux Libraires	22
Cour d'Albane	24
Tour S. Romain	27, 29
The West Front	28
Tour de Beurre	30
Portail de la Calende	31
CHAPTER III.—THE INTERIOR	35
The Nave	35
The Organ	40
South Aisle of Nave	40
La Chapelle du Petit S. Romain	41
South Transept	42
North Transept	43
The Library	44
The Treasury	45
North Aisle of Nave	45
The Choir	46
The Sacristy	47
The Lady Chapel	49
Monuments	49
The Choir Stalls	56

CONTENTS.

THE ABBEY CHURCH OF ST. OUEN.

	PAGE
CHAPTER I.—HISTORY OF THE BUILDING	61
CHAPTER II.—THE EXTERIOR	73
North-West Tower	73
South-West Tower	75
South Transept	75
The Chevet	79
North Transept	83
Tour aux Clercs	83
CHAPTER III.—THE INTERIOR	87
The Vaulting	88
The Nave	91
The Organ Gallery	95
The Priest's Chamber	95
Tour aux Clercs	95
The Choir	96

ST. MACLOU.

CHAPTER I.—HISTORY OF THE BUILDING	101
CHAPTER II.—THE EXTERIOR	106
CHAPTER III.—THE INTERIOR	113
AÎTRE DE S. MACLOU	114

APPENDIX I.—DIMENSIONS OF THE THREE CHURCHES	119
APPENDIX II.—THE MINOR CHURCHES OF ROUEN	120
St. Gervais	120
St. Paul	120
St. Vincent	121
St. Patrice	121
St. Laurent	121
St. Goddard	122
St. Nicaise	122
St. Vivien	122
St. Romain	122

ILLUSTRATIONS.

	PAGE
Rouen Cathedral from the Pont Corneille	*Frontispiece*
Arms of the City of Rouen	*Title Page*

CATHEDRAL CHURCH OF NOTRE DAME.

West Front	6
La Chapelle de la Haute Vielle Tour	9
The Butter Tower from the West	15
Portail aux Libraires	20
Panels on the Portail aux Libraires	23
Statues in the Court of the Portail aux Libraires	24
Cour d'Albane	25
Base of the Tour St. Romain	26
Carving on the North-West Doorway	29
The Butter Tower	30
Portail de la Calende	31
Nave from the West	34
South Arcading of the Nave	36
South Aisle	38
The Lantern	39
Chapel of St. Stephen	41
Staircase to the Library	44
The Choir	47
The Sacristy	48
The Lady Chapel from the East	50
Monuments of Pierre and Louis de Brézé	51
Monument of the two Cardinals d'Amboise	53
Remains of the Abbey of St. Amand	54
Tomb of Archbishop Maurice	56
The Choir from the South Aisle of the Nave	57

ILLUSTRATIONS.

THE ABBEY CHURCH OF ST. OUEN.

	PAGE
St. Ouen from the North-West	60
North Transept	65
West Front	67
View from the North-East	72
The South Side	74
South Transept	76
Portail des Marmosets	77
Part of the Chevet	80
Flying Buttresses of the Choir	81
Tour aux Clercs	83
The Nave	86
South Aisle	90
The West End of the Nave	91
View from North Aisle of Nave, looking into the Choir	92
From the Triforium of the North Transept	93
The Choir	96
Iron Doors of Choir	98

ST. MACLOU.

Organ Staircase	100
West Front	102
Tympanum of West Door	107
Part of West Door	109
View of Interior from the West	112
Aître S. Maclou	115
Plan of St. Ouen } Plan of the Cathedral }	*end*

THE CHURCHES OF ROUEN.

INTRODUCTION.

FEW cities of the same size can vie with Rouen in the beauty of its churches. None in England possessing a cathedral can at the present day boast also of an abbey church with dimensions scarcely if at all inferior. In Rouen, however, we have the cathedral church of Notre Dame, and the abbey church of St. Ouen, which the majority of visitors assert to exceed it in beauty, and many other churches with which it would be beyond the scope of this book to deal.

Three churches have been chosen for special description in this volume. 1. The cathedral church of **Notre Dame,** which from the earliest days has been the seat of an archbishop, and which, like most of our English cathedral churches, but unlike many of those in France, shows work of all ages, and in all styles that have prevailed from the twelfth century to the present time. 2. The church of **St. Ouen,** which from its foundation until the time of the first French Revolution, was the church of a Benedictine community, and which as it stands to-day is marked by a singular unity of design. The choir and transepts were erected in twenty-one years (1318–1339), and though the nave was not finished until the early part of the sixteenth century, it seems to have been erected, as far as its general features are concerned, in accordance with the original design. The central tower is considerably later than the transept from which it rises, and dates from the latter half of the fifteenth century. St. Ouen may be well regarded as in its conception an almost perfect specimen of the very finest period of Gothic architecture—the fourteenth century. The eastern part shows work actually done at this period: in the western part of the church and in the central tower we may mark the signs of the transition to the Flamboyant style, which was contemporaneous with our English Perpendicular.

3. The church of **St. Maclou**, the finest of the purely parish churches of Rouen, presenting nothing older than work of the Flamboyant period, but unfortunately marred in the interior by Renaissance work.

Comparing the two larger churches, Notre Dame and St. Ouen, with our English cathedrals, we find that they do not differ from the ordinary English type to such an extent as many French cathedrals do. This may possibly be largely due to the fact that Rouen is in Normandy, a duchy which was for a century and a half ruled by one who wore the English crown as well as the Norman coronet, and which even after this time, especially in the early part of the fifteenth century, was largely under English influence.

The general characteristic differences between French and English churches of cathedral rank are that the former are higher, broader, shorter, that they have apsidal terminations at the east end, and that their towers are far less important features, the height of the nave roof dwarfing the proportions of the tower or spire, even though it be of considerable height. That their doorways, especially the western ones, are grander both in size and richness of decoration. Comparing the two large churches of Rouen with English examples, we find that they are each roughly 450 feet in length, about the same as Salisbury; in width the nave of Salisbury is 82 feet including the aisles, St. Ouen 84 feet, and Notre Dame, including the chapels, 105 feet. So that in proportion of length to breadth these two churches do not differ greatly from Salisbury, which may be considered as a typical English example. But in height the nave of St. Ouen exceeds even that of Westminster Abbey by a few feet, and is a quarter as high again as Salisbury. The central space between the arcading, which divides the nave proper from its aisles, is rather less than at Salisbury, so that, as usual in French cathedrals, the proportion of height to width is greater than in the English example. The nave of Notre Dame is lower, and as its width is not very different from that of St. Ouen, its proportions more nearly approach those of the English type, though the height here also is somewhat greater in proportion to the width than in any English building save Westminster, which in design shows traces of French influence. Each of these two churches at Rouen has the usual French east end with its apsidal ambulatory and series of radiating chapels on the outside. The towers of Notre Dame and St. Ouen have as much importance as those of our English cathedrals. The western towers of Notre Dame are nearly as high as the central tower of Lincoln, and surpass in height all the western cathedral towers in England; while the central tower, apart from the cast-iron spire, which rises nearly 100 feet higher into the air than our loftiest English spire, is somewhat lower than the western towers; but as it was always intended to be crowned with a spire of some kind, it must always have held its own amid its neighbours. The central tower of St. Ouen surpasses in height the central tower of Lincoln by about ten feet, so that although the nave of St. Ouen is about twenty feet higher than that of Lincoln, the tower is not dwarfed, but is a distinctly imposing feature. The western spires, nineteenth century work, are somewhat lower and do not group badly with the central tower. The five large portals of Notre Dame and the six of St. Ouen, of which five are modern, are French in character and dimensions. When we come to compare the two churches, Notre Dame and St. Ouen, together, we find that they differ in many particulars; each has advantages that the other does not possess. St. Ouen has undoubtedly a much better site than Notre Dame. There is ample space all round it from which it may be seen; the only building that in any way impedes the view is the long low classical building abutting upon the north transept now used as the Hotel de Ville, but which before the time of the dissolution of the monastery served as part of the domestic buildings of the monks. This is the first advantage this church possesses over its rival; the second is the unity of design which it presents. All is in perfect harmony; there is nothing that offends the eye at first sight, nothing that seems too large or too small; the proportion of the whole is excellent. The interior, too, is impressive; the vista looking from the west is sufficiently long to bear the height of its vault; but when we begin to examine its details, then its shortcomings begin to be apparent. We find, despite the elaborate carving on its southern frontal and the richness of the central tower, that there are signs of poverty of design. The same tracery is repeated in window after window, though there is a marked difference between the early fourteenth century windows in the eastern part of the church and the later windows of the nave, and there is a certain feeling of coldness inside. The arcading of the nave, the piers of which have no bold general abacus or capital, is by no means rich or satisfactory. The chief merits of the church are enumerated when we say it possesses a splendid site, magnificent size, perfect harmony of parts, and excellent proportion; together with some individual parts marked by beautiful workmanship.

The cathedral is lacking in many of these points in which St. Ouen excels. It is terribly encumbered by surrounding buildings. A good general view of the whole can nowhere be obtained; the open square before the western façade is not sufficiently large to allow one to see the west front to perfection. The streets that run along the northern and southern sides are narrow and winding; the east end is entirely blocked up by the walls of the archbishop's palace. There is no symmetry about the building; the two western towers are of different dates and different design; the modern cast-iron spire placed on the central tower is utterly out of keeping with the rest of the building, and is thin, wire-drawn, and badly proportioned in itself. This church entirely lacks the unity of design that is so marked a feature in that of St. Ouen; but when this has been said all the defects of this beautiful building have been noticed, save perhaps that the four lateral towers have never been finished. We walk round the exterior of the church, examining all that we can see, and we find no sameness, no repetition of features. We enter the church, and here again the constant variety, the evidence of wealth of thought on the part of the builders, strikes us; the form of the windows and their tracery vary, and there is much to be examined in detail. It is a church which has grown up, has been added to, and altered from time to time, and in it we may find work of every age of Gothic art, a thing we in England are accustomed to look for in our cathedral churches, but which cannot so frequently be found on the other side of the Channel. It is richer than St. Ouen in tombs and monuments, and its details are more generally interesting. What is lacking in symmetry and harmony as a whole is more than compensated by the excellence of its parts. The western façade is for the most part mediæval, and marked by a wealth of free work which contrasts favourably with the mechanical regularity of the nineteenth century west front of St. Ouen. But a thorough renovation of the western façade of the cathedral has been undertaken in the present year, so that it is to be feared that it will, when this work is completed, have lost much of its charm. There is much more that demands careful examination in Notre Dame than in St. Ouen; but each church is excellent in its own way, and well deserves the praise that has been bestowed upon it. Well can we understand Fergusson writing: "The church of St. Ouen at Rouen was beyond comparison the most beautiful and perfect of the abbey churches of France. . . . Nothing, indeed, can exceed the beauty of proportion of this most elegant church; and except that it wants the depth and earnestness of the earlier examples, it may be considered as the most beautiful thing of its kind in Europe." Well, too, can we believe that Mr. Ruskin really said on one of the many occasions when he visited this church, as the verger at St. Ouen tells us he did: "This is the finest monument of pure Gothic in the world—too beautiful for a house of prayer. I can never pray in it; I can only look at it without ceasing."

CATHEDRAL CHURCH OF NOTRE DAME, WEST FRONT.

THE CATHEDRAL CHURCH OF NOTRE DAME, ROUEN.

CHAPTER I.

HISTORY OF THE BUILDING.

ROUEN has been an inhabited place throughout all historic time. Before the Roman conqueror led his victorious legions into Northern Gaul, the Keltic hut-dwellers had gathered together on the outside curve of the river beneath the rising ground that encircles the modern city of Rouen on the northeast, and had cast his nets into the waters of the river. Under Cæsar and the early Roman emperors, with its original name of Ratuma or Ratumacos Latinised into Rotomagus, it was the chief town of the Veliocassians, and so continued until, towards the end of the third century, it became the capital of Lugdunensis Secunda, and shortly afterwards the See of an archbishop. Legend speaks of the conversion of the inhabitants to Christianity in the second century by St. Nicaise.

A more real personage, however, was the Cardiff missionary, St. Mellon, who in the year 260 came to preach at Rouen, and afterwards became the first bishop. Among his hearers was one Precordius, so the legend has it, who, seated on the roof of his house, listened until, like Eutychus of old, wearied by the long sermon he was overcome by sleep and fell from the roof to the ground below, and was taken up dead; but as St. Paul had restored Eutychus to life, so did St. Mellon restore Precordius, and the first Christian Church was established in his house. The body of St. Mellon was many years after his death laid in the crypt beneath the Church of St. Gervais, perhaps the oldest relic of Christian art in Northern France, built by St. Victrice, the seventh archbishop, to receive the relics of St. Gervais. In this crypt St. Mellon's tomb may still be seen, but his body was dug up by the Protestants when they ravaged the city in 1562. Here, too, was deposited the body of the second bishop, St. Avitien, who had died in 325, and who had raised on the foundations of the rude and primitive church of St. Mellon a building more worthy of being a Christian place of worship; this served for St. Leon, Avitien's immediate successor, and the other bishops until about the year 400, when St. Victrice, the sixth successor of St. Mellon, entirely reconstructed the church on the site of the present Cathedral of Notre Dame. Whether the churches of St. Mellon and St. Avitien occupied the same site is uncertain.

It is said that the first church on the site of the existing church of St. Ouen was founded about the same time. But all this early Christian work has disappeared, save the underground Chapel of St. Gervais built as above-mentioned by St. Victrice, probably after his journey to Rome in 404, during which he received from St. Ambrose of Milan certain portions of the body of St. Gervais, whose wonder-working powers he hoped might strengthen the faith of his little congregation in the north, and add to its number fresh converts from heathenism. In 488 St. Godard was elected fourteenth bishop, and he represented his diocese when Hlodowig or Clovis was baptised at Rheims.

In the seventh century St. Romain, the nineteenth archbishop, who died in 638, enlarged the church. Connected with his name is the curious privilege enjoyed by the cathedral chapter, by which they had the right to release on each Ascension Day a prisoner condemned to death, who had to raise on his shoulders and carry in solemn procession "La fierte St. Romain"—a shrine containing the relics of the saint—from the chapel of St. Romain to the cathedral. A shrine thus used may still be seen in the cathedral treasury, and the "chapelle de la fierte[1] de St. Romain," where the pardoned prisoner received the shrine, still stands in the "Place de la haute vielle Tour." The present chapel, built about 1542, is not the original, but its Renaissance

---

[1] Fierte is probably derived from the Latin feretrum—a bier.

HISTORY OF THE BUILDING.

successor, just as the shrine now shown was not the one used in the earliest times. A list of the names of the prisoners released from 1210 to 1790 is still preserved. This document gives an account of the crimes for which each had been condemned to death, and throws an interesting light upon the manners and customs of mediæval times.

The legend told about the origin of this privilege, which, though fully believed in for many years, was only of late growth, no mention of it having been made until some 700 years after the supposed performance of the miracle, is this:—The people of Rouen suffered, as did the inhabitants of many other mediæval towns, from the depredations of a certain dragon. The dragon, who devastated the neighbourhood of Rouen, bore the name of Gargouille; from her lair in the reedy swamps beside the river she came out to devour the inhabitants of the city. St. Romain, however, took a condemned criminal, and using him as a bait, enticed the dragon from her den, and then by the use of the holy sign subdued the monster to his will, and tying the end of his stole round its neck, led it into the city, where it was slain and its body burnt amid the rejoicings of the people. To commemorate this deliverance, it is said that the king granted the Privilege de St. Romain above described, to the cathedral chapter. We need not be surprised to learn from the legend that the saint restored life and soundness of limb and body to the criminal whom he had used as a bait, and that the criminal, on account of his part in the deliver-

LA CHAPELLE DE LA HAUTE VIELLE TOUR.

ance that had been wrought, was set at liberty. But the legend was an aftergrowth invented to explain a custom which really had a different origin. It appears that the release of a prisoner was in some way connected with one of the Miracle Plays performed on Ascension Day, and that the privilege was first exercised about the middle of the twelfth century. We find our Henry VI. in 1425 ordering an enquiry into this privilege, for in that year the chapter had selected a Frenchman who had killed an Englishman, as the criminal who was to be pardoned. It was only in the year 1512 that the privilege, which had hitherto been a custom, received legal confirmation from Louis XII., and at this time the Gargouille legend of its origin was only vaguely mentioned.

St. Ouen, who died in 683, is said to have embellished the cathedral, but of his work no trace remains. For the country suffered from other devastators than the fabled Gargouille, for as upon England so on Northern France, the Norse pirates who first appeared in the year 841 began to make raids in summer time; and after a while, finding the climate so much pleasanter than that of their northern home, began to stay through the winter months as well. The same plans of getting rid of the invaders were tried in France as in England: force of arms sometimes accomplished for a time what was desired, and when that failed, gold wherewith to induce them to depart was given them, with the natural result that they came again next year for more. All efforts to get permanently rid of the invaders failed, and before the end of the ninth century, Hrolf, Rollo, Rollon or Rou, as his name variously appears, was recognised as ruler of Normandy by the Carolingian king, became the king's man, married his daughter, and like Guthrum in England, embraced Christianity, being baptised by the Archbishop of Rouen in the year 912. This was the foundation of the Norman Duchy.

The Norsemen, however, had not found Rouen in a flourishing condition when they began to plunder. A great fire had swept away much of the city in 556, after this came a plague, and in the confusion that followed the reign of Charles the Great, Rouen still further suffered. Thus Rollo had, as it were, to found a new capital as well as a new dynasty. He built a stronghold, drained the reed beds, and, what was of more importance, encouraged learning, welcoming to his capital men renowned for their skill in art and song, and ecclesiastics famed for their theological knowledge. The cathedral was enlarged by him, and in 930 his body was laid to rest within its walls, the first layman who had ever received the honour of burial within the church; here, too, was laid the body of his son William Longsword, murdered in 943, though during his lifetime he had been at heart more of a heathen than a Christian. These tombs are still pointed out, one in a chapel on the south side of the nave, the other in one on the north side, though these cannot have been the original places of interment, as these chapels were added to the church much later. To him succeeded Richard the Fearless, who, during his long rule of 53 years, still further enlarged the cathedral, and repaired its floor. His son Robert was forty-third archbishop of Rouen. The long dreaded time was now drawing near when it was thought that the world would perish in fervent heat, and terror possessed the minds of men. The days indeed were evil, and safety seemed only to be hoped for within the walls of the churches, where vast congregations of men, women, and children were gathered together to wait the end. But the fatal time drew near, came, and passed away, and nothing happened; and when the world was fairly through the critical period, men breathed freely once more. Casting aside their fear, they began with exuberance of joy to take an interest in mundane matters once again. One of the forms their new energy took was that of building; and hence the eleventh century marked the beginning of a new era in architecture; wood as a building material gave place to stone, and from this century date some of the oldest existing remains of mediæval architecture in France as well as in England.

One difference between the origin of the great English and French churches must be noticed. In England they were built chiefly at the expense of ecclesiastical bodies, who derived their property from various sources: royal grants of land, gifts made by nobles who, looking back upon their lawless lives often stained by bloodshed and disgraced by other crimes, felt uneasy about their future in another world, and so strove to make their peace with heaven by gifts to the Church. In France, however, the churches were in great measure built from funds given by the citizens or burghers, who took a pride in the splendour of their buildings.

The churches were thus as much the work of the civilian as of the ecclesiastic; the various trade guilds left their mark upon the buildings. We see on the walls not only carvings of the saint and the bishop, but also of the mason and the carpenter, the labourer and the merchant. Hence too, perhaps, it came about that whereas in England the cathedral church stands as a rule isolated from the city within its walled enclosure, and with its close of well-kept turf, which adds such a charm to the building, and throws over it such a feeling of peace, the French church stands amid the bustling life of the city; houses, in many cases, now, as formerly, abut upon the walls, the market is held beneath its shadow, stalls are erected close to its portals. At Rouen, for instance, we find the entrance to the north transept called "Le Portail aux Libraires," from the booksellers' stalls that used to be erected there, and a flower market is still held in front of the south transept. The church in France was, far more than in England, the church of the people. Into its cool aisles and naves the weary worker could pass for rest and prayer; he could feel that he had an inheritance therein; he had a sense of property in its soaring roof and "storied windows richly dight," for had not his ancestors and kindred taken part in its erection? There on the carved walls and on the painted windows he could read the lessons that the Church wished to teach him: stories from the Old and New Testaments, and from the lives of holy men and saintly women, from the record of whose deeds he might learn how to guide his steps safely through this sinful world of crime and tyranny and suffering, to another where the oppressor would oppress no more, and where the weary soul would be at rest. The religious temper in those days of old was very different from that of the nineteenth century. Yet even now one may see the market-woman leaving her basket unguarded but safe upon the steps of the church, and kneeling before the image of saint or virgin, and the little children coming in alone and offering up their childish prayers to their favourite saint.

But the church was not only a place of prayer, it was used for various other purposes. Hither, before setting out on some expedition, the warrior would come to receive the blessing of the Church upon his arms; hither would he come again to return thanks if he came back crowned with victory. Grand processions would on solemn occasions pass up the nave or aisles and round the ambulatory or semicircular path that ran between the high altar and the chapels that clustered round the apse. In the nave itself or before the vast western portals, miracle plays and mysteries would be performed. Here, too, when occasion required it, the citizens would meet for civil and sometimes for military purposes. In those old days, religion counted for more than it does now in the lives of the people; there was no doubt in men's minds about the truth of the doctrines taught by the Church, however much the lust of gain and power might lead them at times to forget its teaching. Moreover, in those days there was a love of art that has long since ceased to exist. What does the modern man on the street care for the artistic beauty of his surroundings? Little enough. He may be struck by the vast size or magnificence of some building, but real artistic taste he has none. But in the Middle Ages, if men did not know as much as we know now about sanitary science, yet they liked to live in houses whose outward appearance it was a joy to look upon, and which each had an individuality of its own; and round the Gothic church clustered the Gothic dwelling-houses all in keeping with each other; the church being, indeed, the most magnificent of the buildings in the town, the one object on which the craftsman lavished the best of his skill, the rich man his money, and the master-builder his thoughts. Nowhere did this feeling show itself more thoroughly than in France. There was a rivalry, too, between the various towns; each tried to outdo its neighbours in the splendour, size, and beauty of its public buildings. The democratic spirit fostered by the Commune found its outlet in works in which all might take part. In England, on the other hand, the churches were more fully the work of ecclesiastics, and their fabrics often the property of the special religious bodies that erected them. The laity were often only admitted on sufferance.

But to return from these general observations to the story of the building of the cathedral at Rouen. It has been already stated that great building-works were carried on during the eleventh century; to such an extent, indeed, was this the case that it was practically a new building which was ready for consecration in 1063 A.D. On October 1st of that year the new church was dedicated to the Virgin by Archbishop Maurilius in the presence of William, Duke of Normandy, who was so soon to become famous for his conquest of England. In the year 1079 A.D. the forty-eighth Archbishop of Rouen, Guillaume Bonne Ame, in splendid procession, in which Duke William and his wife Matilda, now King and Queen of England as well as Duke and Duchess of Normandy, took part, bore in a beautiful new shrine the relics of St. Romain, who had been already dead for more than 440 years, from the Church of St. Godard to the new Cathedral Church of Our Lady. So greatly had the fame of the saint grown that St. Godard's church was all too strait to hold the pilgrims who flocked to worship at his shrine. On this occasion the "Foire du Pardon" was instituted, and possibly this gave rise to the subsequently introduced privilege of St. Romain which has been already spoken of. In 1124 A.D. the shrine that held the remains of St. Romain was opened in the presence of the King and Queen of England, Henry I. and Matilda, and in 1178 A.D. a new and more magnificent shrine to contain the sacred relics was made by Archbishop Rotrou. But this, too, has perished.

The lower part of the north-western tower, which bears the name of St. Romain, is all that remains of the eleventh century church, for, with the exception of this, the whole building was destroyed by fire in 1200 A.D. In France and England alike fire seems to have worked its will on many buildings of Norman construction. This was probably due to the timber roofs which were universally used in the buildings of this early date, for not yet had the builders learnt the mechanical principles required to support a wide and lofty vault of stone. We cannot say for certain when the rebuilding of Rouen Cathedral was taken in hand, but probably no great length of time was allowed to pass before measures were taken to make good the damage. From this time up to the sixteenth century, work on this church seems constantly to have been going on; repairs, often extensive, have also been carried out in subsequent centuries. It will now be well to enumerate, with approximate dates, the chief pieces of work as they were done. According to Viollet le Duc the earliest parts of the rebuilt church were

HISTORY OF THE BUILDING. 15

the chapels of the apse, those of the transepts, and the two lateral doors of the western façade; the choir seems also to have been

THE BUTTER TOWER FROM THE WEST
From a Drawing by John Ruskin.

finished before the influence of French Gothic imported from the Isle de France had made itself felt. Enguerrand or

Ingelramus was, according to the *Chronique du Bec*, the architect who designed the new church, but a certain Jean d'Andeli is also spoken of in the chapter-house accounts as a master mason. To Enguerrand succeeded Durand le Machon, then Gautier de St. Hilaire, and then Jean Davi, to whom is due the Portail aux Libraires built in 1278.

In the next century the chapels between the buttresses of the nave were built; and Jean de Bayeux is found among the few builders whose names have been preserved. Jean Salvart superintended the work during the reign of Henry V. of England, and enlarged the choir windows. Jean Roussel carried on the work from 1430 till 1452, when he was succeeded by Geoffroi Richier. In 1463 Guillaume Pontifz took charge of the work and carried it on for no less than 34 years, during which the Portail de la Calende was finished, the upper part of the Tour St. Romain added, the sixth stage between 1467 and 1470, and the roof in 1477, the walls of the courtyard in front of the north transept, and the screen that divides it from the Rue St. Romain were erected, the staircase in the north transept leading up to the library and treasury built, and the Tour de Beurre commenced. This tower received its curious name because the cost of its building was in great measure defrayed by money paid by the people for indulgences which permitted them to eat butter in Lent. The foundation was laid during the episcopate of Robert de Croixmare on November 10th, 1487, and the tower was finished by Jaques le Roux in the time of the great Cardinal Archbishop Georges d'Amboise I. in 1507. Before the tower was finished the archbishop gave 4000 livres to the chapter to pay for the casting of a big bell which was to be hung in the tower when finished. This bell was successfully cast by Jehan le Machon on August 2nd, 1501, was hung on October 9th of the same year, and was rung for the first time on February 10th, 1502. The bellfounder did not live to hear his masterpiece rung, for he died twenty-six days after the casting of the bell.

On the bell was the following inscription:—

> Je suis nommée Georges d'Amboise :
> Qui bien trente-six mille poise :
> Et cil qui bien me poisera,
> Quarante mille trouvera.

It measured 30 feet in circumference, 13 in height, and

HISTORY OF THE BUILDING.

over 8 inches in thickness. Its tone was not what might have been expected from so large a bell; it, however, hung in the Butter Tower, and was rung until, on the 26th day of June 1786, when it was being rung in honour of the entry of Louis XVI. into Rouen it was cracked, an evil omen of coming disaster to the ill-fated king. The metal of the great bell was melted by the republicans in 1793, and most of it used for the casting of cannons. Some was converted into medals, bearing the inscription:

>"Monument de Vanité
>Détroit pour l'utilité
>L'an deux de l'égalité."

The chapel at the base of the Butter Tower dedicated to St. Stephen, which served as a parish church, was consecrated on May 14th, 1496.

In 1508 the ornamentation of the western façade was commenced by Rouland Leroux, and finished in 1527. The names of the carvers of the statues are preserved, viz., Pierre Dalix, Hance de Bony, Denis Lerebours, Nicholas Quesnel, and Jean Theroulde, and another sculptor who bore the same name as the architect, while Pierre Desaubeaulx carved the central tympanum.

The central tower of the eleventh century church was terminated by a pyramidal roof of wood. This was struck by lightning in 1117 and burnt. After the great fire in 1200 a new central tower was built crowned with a spire, which was burnt on October 4th, 1514. The tower was then raised another stage of about 36 feet, and on it was placed a wooden spire whose top reached the height of 430 feet from the ground. This spire was built by Robert Becquet, finished in 1550, and lasted till 1822, when, like one of its predecessors, it was set on fire by a flash of lightning and destroyed. This disaster occurred on September 15th. In the following year, plans for the present iron spire were commenced by the architect Alavoine, and the work of erecting it was begun in 1827. His aim was to raise the spire to a still greater height than the old one, and in this he succeeded, as the vane on the top reaches a height of close upon 500 feet; its weight is about a million and a quarter pounds. The spire is not coated with lead, but is of open iron work, through which the sky can be seen.

About 48 feet from the summit there is an awkward excrescence, having somewhat the appearance of a bird cage, which breaks the symmetry of the tapering spire. Much has been said, and justly said, against this addition to the central tower, but seen from a distance it seems to pull together the composition of the pile; and as architectural purists are always finding fault with architects for making slavish copies of ancient work, and bidding them to put up frankly modern work in any additions that they make, there are some who will not feel inclined to join to the full in the chorus of abuse which has been lavished on Alavoine's work. The nineteenth century may be well regarded as an iron age. The iron spire of Rouen, therefore, marks an epoch: it is characteristic of the time of its erection and cannot possibly be mistaken for sixteenth century work. With the erection of this spire the history of the building of Notre Dame may be said to conclude, and until quite recent times the church had escaped the ordinary fate of cathedrals, namely, restoration. Its walls bore the mark of age; the carving of the western façade, though much weathered, had the charm that the mellowing hand of time gives; in the crevices between the stones, vegetable growth set by the hand of nature might be seen among man's imitation of natural forms; but now all this is changed. Scaffolding, at the time of the writer's last visit to Rouen in May 1900, concealed the greater part of the magnificent west front; white glaring stonework might be seen let into the old work, hoary with age, blackened by rain and sun; masons were busy in the Cour d'Albane carving crockets and finials, which in due time would be hoisted up to take their place on the west front; and there is reason to fear that, when the scaffolding comes down, much of the charm which the façade wore a few years ago will have vanished.

With a few words about the bells of Notre Dame this chapter dealing with the history of the building must now be brought to a conclusion. The story of the great bell Georges d'Amboise in the Tour de Beurre has already been told. In the central tower there were once four bells which were rung to give notice to the canons of the hours of service; these perished in the fire of 1514. Four new bells were almost at once hung in their places; these were in 1794 melted by the Revolutionists. A new set was hung after the Concordat, but these perished in the fire of 1822.

HISTORY OF THE BUILDING.

In the sixth stage of the Tour St. Romain there was formerly a peal of eleven bells, but in 1686 the number was reduced to eight, four bells being melted down, and from the metal of which they had been composed one new bell was cast. Among these four was one named Guillaume d'Estouteville, the gift of the cardinal whose name it bore. To the new bell of 1686 were given the names of le Bourdon, le Quatre-une, la Reunie, or la d'Estouteville. It weighed 6000 kilograms, was two metres in height, and required six men to ring it. It was the only bell that escaped at the time of the Revolution, but it was cracked in 1845. In 1810 to this one remaining bell Cardinal Cambacérès, Archbishop of Rouen, added two others: the Petite Marie, which had been cast in 1774, and the Jean Baptist, which had been cast in 1785. In 1825 the number of the peel was made up to four by the addition of a bell named Caroline, after the Duchess of Berry. The new bell that has taken the place of the one cracked in 1845 weighs 7500 kilogrammes. This same tower contains the cathedral clock.

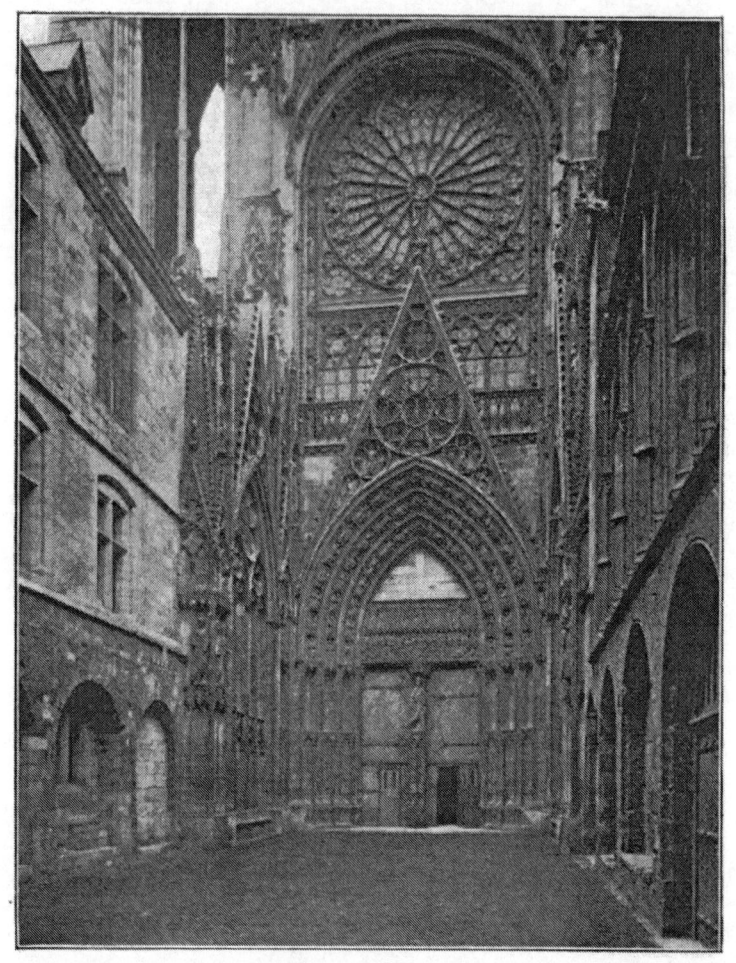

PORTAIL AUX LIBRAIRES.

CHAPTER II.

THE EXTERIOR.

THE Cathedral Church of Notre Dame is so blocked in with buildings that it is difficult from any point to obtain a satisfactory view of it taken as a whole. The three towers may be seen well from the Pont Corneille, but from this point of view the body of the church is hidden by the buildings along the quay on the north side of the river. Possibly a better idea of the size and general character of the church may be obtained by ascending to the roof of St. Ouen, from which point of view the upper part of the walls, the flying buttresses, and the roofs of the cathedral, that above the choir green from verdigris, for the roof is of copper, may be seen rising above the roofs of the intervening houses. The west front with its three imposing portals, the central one surmounted with a lofty pediment or gable of delicate tracery, its magnificent rose window, its tiers of statues, its two vast towers rising approximately to the same height but of different ages, character, and design, its four turrets, two crowned with spires, rows of arcading, open tracery and tiers of statues may fortunately be seen from the open space to the west known as the Place Notre Dame. The southern side of the cathedral, from which houses which are represented in an engraving of fifty years ago built close against the nave have been cleared away, can even now only be seen from a narrow street; but opposite to the end of the south transept, an open space, the Place de la Calende, is met with, the level of which slopes rapidly to the south, and which is frequently occupied by the stalls of a flower market; from this a good view of the south transept doorway and the two towers flanking the transept may be obtained. Eastward of this the street again is narrow, and the east end is entirely blocked in by houses and the archiepiscopal residence. The north side is also blocked in; the palace walls hide the view entirely as one passes from the east until the entrance to the court opposite the Portail aux Libraires is reached; from this the north transept is well seen, but again to the west of this gateway the narrow street of St. Romain is flanked on the south side by houses which entirely shut out all sight of the church; however, by entering under a weathered archway on the north side of the Tour St. Romain, the Cour d'Albane is reached, and from this the north side of the nave, the west side of the north transept, and the central tower and spire can be well seen.

Our examination of the exterior may be conveniently commenced at the **Portail aux Libraires.** The court before it is divided from the Rue St. Romain by an outer gateway with two openings. This was built in 1481 by Guillaume Pontifz. On either side of the courtyard are buildings; those on the left were once used as prisons for persons convicted of ecclesiastical offences, and the upper stories of those on the right are the library and treasury of the cathedral. On the ground floor resides the attendant who has charge of the central tower. The court itself was once used as a cemetery, but its use for this purpose was abandoned after it had been desecrated by murder. Rows of booksellers' shops or stalls once occupied the sides of the courtyard. In the fifteenth century there were twelve such shops let by the chapter at the annual rent of sixty livres each. The "portail" or doorway was built for Archbishop Guillaume de Flavacourt in 1278 by Jean Davi, and is worth careful examination, owing to the beauty of the carving. Under the three main niches on either side of the doorway there are three square pedestals, set diagonally, and a similar one may be seen in the centre between the two doors. On each of the two outer faces of these are carved five quatrefoiled panels or medallions, while another series runs up either side of the doorway; and others may be seen on two similar pedestals, on each of the side walls. Each medallion is carved in bas-relief; at the corner of each is some grotesque animal. Mr. Ruskin chooses one of these panels for description in *The Seven Lamps of Architecture,* p. 172, to show "the evidence of thoughtfulness

THE EXTERIOR.

and fancy which is not common, at least nowadays." He points out the expression in the faces of the creatures; in one he notes "in the peculiarly reverted eye the expression which is never seen but in the eye of a dog gnawing something in jest, and preparing to start away with it"; in another, an expression "of gloomy and angry brooding." "The plan of this head," he says, "and the nod of the cap over the brow are fine, but there is a little touch above the hand especially well meant: the fellow is vexed and puzzled in his malice, and his hand is pressed hard on his cheek bone, and the flesh of the cheek is wrinkled under the eye by the pressure." He also bids us look at the tracery and mouldings in detail, for this doorway marks, in his opinion, the culminating point of French Gothic. Above the pedestals just mentioned are niches with their canopies on a level with the spring of the arch of the doorway. Round the head of this doorway are three lines of carved figures, saints and angels, one above another. The

PANELS ON THE PORTAIL AUX LIBRAIRES.

tympanum was never finished, the upper part is left blank, but below it are two tiers of carving, the lower representing the Resurrection of the Last Day; the upper the Judgment. On the pedestal between the two doors stands a restored statue of St. Romain leading Gargouille by his stole. Above the doorway is a gable with open tracery; on its summit stands a statue of an angel, behind it a gallery and a great window, the upper part of which takes the form in which French builders so much delighted—a wheel or rose; above this is another gable with open tracery. On either side of the transept at the N.E. and N.W. corners stands a tower which has never been completed. The upper stories of these towers are open, the tall openings having a pointed arch at the top comprising two sub-arches supported by a slender banded central shaft, the space between their heads being pierced by a sixfoil opening, figured on Plate III. of *The Seven Lamps of Architecture* as an illustration of the development of window tracery. These towers are at present finished above with a parapet pierced with quatrefoil openings. There can be little doubt that it was intended that from within this parapet a spire should rise, but this has never been built. Had the cathedral ever been completed it would have presented a magnificent appearance with its seven towers and spires and clustered pinnacles.

STATUES IN THE COURT OF THE PORTAIL AUX LIBRAIRES.

There is some rich arcading with gables and niches, in some of which statues stand, towards the southern ends of the walls which flank the court leading up to the great doorway just described.

If, on leaving the court, we turn to the left and proceed along the Rue St. Romain to its end, and then turn once more to the left under an archway, we find ourselves in the **Cour d'Albane**, so called from a college for the education of three priests, three deacons, and four sub-deacons, which was founded here in 1245 by Pierre de Colmieu, fifty-fifth Archbishop of Rouen and Cardinal of Albe. Facing us we see some restored windows; these light a chamber running

COUR D'ALBANE.

parallel to but extending beyond the transept, once used as the "Salle capitulaire," but now as a vestry. In this court once stood the Canons' bakehouse, renowned for the excellence of the bread baked therein. Over the vestry are two other stories, the upper with dormer windows in a high-pitched roof. This building joins that seen on the west side of

BASE OF THE TOUR ST. ROMAIN.

the Portail aux Libraires. From this point of view the central tower may be well seen. It stands on a basement of the thirteenth century. Above this is the first stage, which is open to the interior and thus forms a lantern. This is fourteenth and fifteenth century work. It may here be noted that the windows of this stage are divided by transoms crossing the window about midway between the bottom and the spring of the arch. Above this is another stage added in the sixteenth century, on which rises the modern iron spire.

From the north-east corner of the Cour d'Albane the **Tour St. Romain** may be examined. The lowest stage of this is the oldest part of the church, as may be seen by the round-headed windows which are so familiar to us in our Norman churches, but which are not so often met with in Normandy itself. This part of the building escaped the great fire of 1200, which wrought such havoc with the rest of the church. Against the base of this tower stands the porter's lodge. One of the duties of the porter in former times was to guard the prisoners who having committed offences within the jurisdiction of the Chapter were tried in the lodge, and confined in a dungeon below the Tour St. Romain. He also had charge of the watch-dogs that at night-time were let loose inside the church to protect it against attacks of robbers in quest of the various articles of value that might be found within its walls. This method of protecting the church was only abandoned in 1760. A turret containing a staircase stands at the south end of the eastern face of the tower, and runs up to the top of the third stage, and is then capped by a tall pyramidal roof. The two western towers stand respectively to the north and south of the aisles, thus adding considerably to the width of the western façade. Before leaving the Cour d'Albane, which is at present used as a stone-masons' yard by the men employed in the restoration of the west front now in progress, it will be well to notice the windows of the chapels built between the buttresses of the aisles. They are not all alike; for while they bear a general resemblance to each other, there is a great variety in the details of the tracery, resembling in this respect the windows at Exeter, though their great height gives them a dignity not to be found in the English example. One other feature is worth notice: over each of the windows is a gable rising at its point above the pierced parapet that crowns the walls of the chapel; along the top of the clerestory walls in like manner runs a pierced parapet.

Leaving the Cour d'Albane we can cross the old parvis now called the Place Notre Dame, where in former times miracle plays were acted, and stand before the beautiful **West Front**.

One cannot but be overwhelmed with the wealth of carving which it displays, not only in the number of separate statues almost past counting (it is said that there are over three hundred of them) but there is a life, an individuality, an evidence of thought about them; they are not mere mechanical carvings done to order, but in each, despite their time-worn condition, we can trace the joy the workman had in his work, the pains he took with it, and how each man put his heart and soul into his work. On the tympanum above the central door may be seen a Tree of Jesse by Desobaulx, and beneath it are Renaissance doors carved by Colin Castile. On the tympanum of the left doorway are sculptured three scenes from the life of John the Baptist, namely, Salome before Herod; the beheading; and the bringing of the head to Salome. On the corresponding tympanum of the right-hand doorway is a carving of Christ in Glory and the Martyrdom of St. Stephen. Between the doorways and on the outside of the outer doors are buttresses carved with many tiers of panels and terminating in richly carved pinnacles. Over the arch of the central doorway rises a gable, with a very acute angle at its apex standing free from the wall behind, with richly carved flamboyant tracery; behind it is the great western window, circular, according to the general custom in France. "There is no feature," says Fergusson, "on which the French architects bestowed more pains, nor in which they were more successful, than in the construction of circular windows, the *chefs-d'œuvre* of their decorative abilities." Over the lateral doorways are sustaining arches, each about a quadrant of a circle in form, over these a tier of arcading. The west front rises into four turrets, rectangular in plan, the two outer ones capped with open spirelets, on the summits of which statues stand; the two others were once no doubt similarly terminated, but these terminations have disappeared. Between these two central turrets, and above the pointed recessed arch that rises over the great rose window, is some open arcading with canopies. The western gable of the nave is richly decorated with pinnacles, and terminates in an open-work pinnacle which bears a cross.

On the north side of the central archway containing the wheel window is an arcading consisting of four arches, some with three, others with four rows of niches, some of which still contain statues. The heads of the arches are decorated with

THE EXTERIOR.

various forms of flamboyant tracery, the second from the centre standing free with no wall behind it. There are three similar arches on the southern side of the central window, but the head of the middle one has perished. Here, as elsewhere in the church, the great diversity of forms employed is worthy of all admiration. The western front in general appearance, save in the two great towers, possesses perfect symmetry, but the details are different.[1] The first stage of the north-west tower, that of **St. Romain**, is plain; a buttress, whose bottom dies away in the wall of the first stage, runs up the tower to the top. In the second stage there are two double blocked-up windows with pointed heads. On the third stage, again, there are two similar windows. In the fourth the windows are higher and richer. In the fifth stage each window consists of two lights divided by a slender shaft enclosed beneath one comprising arch; above these there is a series of machicolations, and above these a pierced parapet.

CARVING ON THE NORTH-WEST DOORWAY.

This was the original termination of the tower, but in the fifteenth century another stage was added. Each face of this stage contains four lofty windows

---

[1] In the description just given of the west front, I have been obliged to have recourse to photographs taken before the restoration at present going on was commenced. This scaffolding now erected has prevented me from photographing the various parts of this side of the building. A negative of one small piece of carving, however, at the lower part of the north-west doorway I was able to secure, and a reproduction from this may be seen in the accompanying illustration.—T. P.

with pointed heads; these windows are furnished with louvre boards; within it the great bell is hung. This stage is terminated above with a pierced parapet with pinnacles, and within this parapet rises a wedge-shaped roof erected in 1477, on the summit of which stand a pair of tall iron crosses enriched with gilt ornaments. To the south of this tower is a plain wall with a pierced parapet, beyond this the first of the four rectangular turrets already described.

The south-western tower, known as the **Tour de Beurre**, is composed of three parts. The first has three stages with two windows in each face save the lowest, of which only two faces have windows. This lower portion is surmounted by an open gallery. The middle portion of the tower consists of one stage only, with two double windows in each face. Above this stage runs another gallery; the upper portion is octagonal in plan, and rises within the pinnacles which terminate the stage just below; its top ends in a rich pinnacled and pierced parapet. The form and character of this tower will be understood by reference to the accompanying illustration, taken from the Place de la Calende on the south side of the building. The south side of the nave bears a general resemblance to the north side, and in like manner the south transept is similar in its features to the

THE BUTTER TOWER.

THE EXTERIOR. 31

north, but there is no court corrèsponding to that before the Portail aux Libraires.

PORTAIL DE LA CALENDE.

The south doorway, known as the **Portail de la Calende**, gains in impressiveness from the fact that it is on a higher level than the ground outside, and is approached by a flight of nine steps. The tympanum is here completely carved with representations of incidents in the life of Christ. The annunciation of the birth of John to Zacharias; Jesus appearing to Mary Magdalene in the form of a gardener; the calling of the apostles; the betrayal by Judas; Peter cutting off the ear of Malchus; the scourging; the way of the cross; and, above all, the crucifixion. In the side niches are statues of the apostles with their emblems. The gable over the doorway is crowned by a statue of Christ. The wheel window cannot be compared, so far as its tracery goes, with the corresponding one on the north transept. It is distinctly ugly, taking the form, as will be seen from the illustration, of a series of ordinary two-light decorated windows set alternately "heads and tails" round the central circle; the interstices are awkwardly filled up by triangles with curved sides. Above the window is a gable similar to that on the north side; on it are carved representations of Christ and the Virgin escorted by four angels who conduct her to heaven.

On one of the panels on the pedestals is a carving of a man who is being hanged. This no doubt represents Pharaoh's chief baker, but it has given rise to a legend, that the cost of this doorway was defrayed by the sale of the confiscated goods of a baker convicted of using false weights, who was hung for this offence. From the chapter registers we learn that the Portail de la Calende was built at the cost of a burgher of Harfleur named Gorrein.

It is said that this entrance to the cathedral was called the Portail de la Calende from a brotherhood of that name, but some authorities derive the name from certain ecclesiastical meetings held here on the first days of four months of the year. An older name for the Place de la Calende was Port Morant; for it was said that in old days the Seine extended over the low ground to the south of the cathedral, and that ships discharged their cargoes here.

To the east of the Place de la Calende runs a narrow street, along the northern side of which may be seen the walls and basements of the chapels that cluster round the choir and apse; but owing to its narrowness and its low level no good views of the building can be obtained here.

To the east of the apse may be seen the entrance to the archbishop's palace. This palace was built by the Cardinals

THE EXTERIOR.

d'Estouteville and Georges d'Amboise I., and therefore dates from the end of the fifteenth and the beginning of the sixteenth centuries. The thrust of the vaulted roof, as is usual in French cathedrals, is opposed by a system of flying buttresses, but these are of a very simple character; abutting against the clerestory, they spring with one arch across the sloping roof of the aisles, and rest upon the buttresses built outside the walls of the aisles proper. These buttresses, however, owing to chapels having been built in the spaces between them, do not visibly project beyond the walls, which, seen from the exterior, might be taken for the walls of the aisle, but are really the walls of the inserted chapels. The tops of these external buttresses are loaded with large low pinnacles, in canopied niches of which statues may be seen.

NAVE FROM THE WEST.

CHAPTER III.

THE INTERIOR—THE NAVE.

WHEN one enters the church by the western door, an unbroken vista meets the eye; the whole interior can be seen, right away to the stilted arches that support the apsidal eastern wall, beneath which may be seen the more distant east window of the Lady Chapel. There is no rood screen to obstruct the view. The choir is merely divided from the crossing by a low iron railing. The chief peculiarity of the interior consists in the arrangement of the arcading dividing the nave from the aisles. In most churches of cathedral or abbey rank we meet with three rows of arches only, the lower ones opening into the aisles, the next into the triforium, which in many cases occupies the space between the vaulting of the aisles and the external lean-to roof of the same; and in other cases, when the aisle roof is gabled, is a simple gallery; and the third contains the clerestory windows. In Notre Dame de Rouen, however, as will be seen from illustration (page 36), there are two tiers of arches in the wall between the nave and aisles. Above the upper row runs the triforium, which is merely a narrow gallery, and above this may be seen the clerestory windows. It will not be necessary to give a verbal description of the arrangement, which will be more easily understood from studying the reproduction of the photograph showing the arcading on the south side. The vaulting will be noticed to be quadripartite. From the base of each pier five vaulting shafts run up in unbroken line to the vaulting; the two exterior ones, which have no capitals, support the longitudinal ribs over the clerestory windows. The next two, which have capitals at the level of the spring of the arch of the clerestory windows, support the diagonal ribs of each compartment; and the remaining shaft, which has a capital at the same level as those on each side of it, supports the transverse vaulting rib.

SOUTH ARCADING OF THE NAVE.

At the crossing of the diagonal ribs there is a boss. The angle at which the transverse ribs from either side meet is a very

SOUTH AISLE.

THE INTERIOR. 39

obtuse one. On passing into the aisles it will be seen that the vaulting has the same general character, but that the angle at which the vaulting ribs meet is rather less obtuse. There is a most curious arrangement of shafts to be seen on the side of the arcading that faces the aisles. From each of the capitals of the main piers which project into the aisle rises a system of free banded shafts terminating in capitals of their own on a

THE LANTERN AS SEEN FROM BELOW.

level with the top of the wall above the lowest tier of arches of the arcading. On this wall stand the shafts from which spring the arches of the upper tier. The system is altogether very complex as will be seen from the illustration opposite, and not very pleasing in appearance. The first stage of the central tower above the roof is open to the crossing, and so forms a lantern.[1] It will be noticed that there is a "dark gallery"

[1] By placing the camera on its back with the lens pointing upward I

running round the lower part of the tower, and above it are the windows, four in each face, arranged in pairs. Eight vaulting ribs spring from shafts at the four angles and at the centres of each face meet in the centre of the roof of the lantern. The same photograph will show the character of the vaulting of the two transepts and the nave.

Commencing from the western entrance it will now be necessary to examine the church in detail.

Over the central door may be seen the **Organ.** Probably the very best position for an organ is that which it formerly occupied in all English cathedral churches and still does in many, namely, in what in pre-Reformation days had been the rood screen which divided the choir from the nave, but the west end seems little if at all inferior. The volume of sound floods the nave, and the effect is very different from that produced in those English churches in which the organ has been removed from the west gallery or rood screen into the choir aisles or an organ chamber.

Notre Dame had an organ in the fourteenth century. In 1493 Archbishop Robert of Croixmare had a new one built. This was rebuilt from 1515–1518, and again enlarged in 1660, but it was much damaged in a terrible storm in 1683 which also did much injury to the western façade. The organ was repaired in 1693. A new one was built in 1790 by one Lefèvre; the present one is by Merklin and Schütze. The organ gallery is classical in character, seventeenth and eighteenth century work.

The first bay on the **south side** is narrow, the next wider; these two are opposite to the Chapel of St. Stephen which occupies the base of the Butter Tower, and was at one time used as a parish church. This chapel is lighted by four windows, three of which are filled with fifteenth century glass. The altar stands against the south wall, behind it is a modern reredos representing the crucifixion, and below it the stoning of St. Stephen.

In the next bay between the buttresses is a chapel lit

endeavoured to secure a photograph of this part of the church which will give the reader some idea of the vaulting. Owing possibly to some unevenness in the floor upon which the camera was placed, the axis of the lens was not exactly vertical at the time the exposure was made. Hence the square base of the tower is seen in angular perspective.—T. P.

by a three-light decorated window containing fifteenth century glass.

In the fourth bay the window has four lights; here, too, is a chapel with an altar, the subject of the reredos is the betrothal of Christ to St. Catherine.

The fifth bay contains an altar and chapel. The window has three lights.

The sixth and seventh bays are also fitted as chapels, and each one is lit by a four-light window.

THE CHAPEL OF ST. STEPHEN.

The eighth bay alone is not fitted as a chapel; there is a four-light decorated window, the lower part of which is encroached on by the head of what was formerly a doorway; this has been blocked up, but a recess in the wall may still be seen.

The ninth bay, again, contains a chapel, and is lit by a four-light window.

The tenth bay contains a chapel known as **"La Chapelle du Petit St. Romain."** It is lit by an exceedingly narrow four-light window. In this chapel is the tomb of Rollo the first Duke of Normandy. The thirteenth century statue on the tomb has been restored. An inscription states, "Here lies Rollo, the first duke, founder, and father of Normandy, of which he was at first the terror and the scourge, but afterwards the restorer. Baptised in 912 by Françon, Archbishop of Rouen; died in 917. His remains were at first deposited in the sanctuary at present the upper end of the nave. The altar having been removed, the remains of the prince were placed here by the blessed Maurille, Archbishop of Rouen, in the year 1063."

This chapel was at one time occupied by the brotherhood of St. Romain, an Order which was founded in 1292 with a view to charitable objects, but which in course of time devoted itself exclusively to the worship of the saint; its changed work was recognised by fresh statutes in 1346. This brotherhood took a prominent part in the ceremony of the "Levée de la Fierte," of which mention has already been made. The members of it carried the shrine of St. Romain to the chapel of the Haute vielle Tour, and they escorted the pardoned prisoner back to the Cathedral as he carried the relics. The master of the brotherhood, after the ceremony was over, gave the prisoner a supper, and the next day a breakfast and a new hat. The master also had charge of the image of Gargouille which played an important part in the procession; he had to keep it in good order, and pay for the decoration of it when it was brought out in public, and also to pay the men who carried it in the procession. The office of master involved no small pecuniary liabilities, hence the wealthiest citizens of Rouen were chosen to fill it. The brotherhood undertook the acting of miracle plays and mysteries and masquerades, and the distribution of wine. By the middle of the eighteenth century, Gargouille had fallen into discredit, and the brotherhood was finally suppressed in 1777. The Cathedral and the Hospital shared the endowments between them. The brotherhood first occupied the chapel mentioned above, but when the number of the members increased it was found too small, and they were allowed to use the chapel of the Innocents, which then took the name of "**La Chapelle du grand St. Romain.**" This is situated in the south-east corner of the south transept.

The **South Transept** has an aisle on the western side lit on the west by two lancet-headed windows, below which runs an arcade of thirteenth century pointed arches furnished with a bench table; this is continued along the south end of the aisle. Above is a window of two plain lancet lights with a circle in the head. Over the great south door at the end of the transept there is some rich arcading. This is partly covered by the wooden interior porch of classical style; above may be seen a window the boundaries of which form an oblong, within which are placed what may be described as four two-light geometrical windows side by side, close together, in their heads quatrefoil openings, and in the spaces between their heads trefoil openings. Over it is a passage with a beautiful pierced arcade, and above this the great wheel window, the tracery of which was described in the preceding chapter. A wide arch to the north and a narrow one to the south divides the transept from the transept aisle. The clerestory has two windows, each consisting of two plain pointed lights with a plain circle in the head. Similar arches separate the transept from its eastern aisle. The triforium arcading has plain lancet heads. At the south end of this aisle is a three light-window which bears some resemblance to the windows to be seen in the period of transition from Decorated to Perpendicular in some English churches. Over the south aisle of the nave, and also over the south aisle of the choir, are four-light windows with foliated heads and ogee tracery.

The altar of St. Romain is seventeenth century work, and of little beauty; but the seventeenth century glass in the window is good, and represents incidents in the life of the saint. Here we may see Benoît and his wife Felinti, the father and mother of Romain, the capture of Gargouille, the flood of the Seine checked by the saint, the miracle of the Holy Oil spilt by the careless priest who dropped the flask containing it; the fragments of the flask were first reunited by St. Romain and then he made the oil flow back into it; the Holy Hand which blessed the saint as he was saying mass, and King Dagobert granting the "Privilege de la Fierte." At the angle between the transept and the choir is an apsidal chapel dedicated to the Holy Ghost.

Before entering the eastern arm of the church it will be best to cross to the **North Transept** and then complete the examination of the nave. The end of the north transept is similar to that of the south, and the aisles are similar; the tracery of the great wheel window is, however, much more pleasing. There are two clerestory windows in the west wall above the aisle, the arched heads of which are wide and low, especially the southern one. At the north end of the west aisle of the transept may be seen the stone staircase leading to the Library and Treasury, which need not be described, as the illustration sufficiently shows its character. It was erected between 1478 and 1480 by order of Cardinal d'Estouteville by G. Pontifz, and carved by Desvignes and Chennevière. It is the square-headed doorway that may be seen at the top which leads into the treasury; the doorway with the arched head below leads only into a large empty chamber in which formerly the books were kept. The collection of books that formed the nucleus of the chapter library was commenced at a very early period, for a catalogue made in the twelfth century and another made in the thirteenth are still in existence. Books were continually added to it by gifts of the archbishops and canons, and in the fifteenth century it had become of such importance that the chapter decided to erect a special building to hold the books. In 1439 a list of the manuscripts was made and statutes drawn up to regulate the use of the books.

STAIRCASE TO THE LIBRARY.

The **Library Building** is that which forms the western side of the court already described between the north transept doorway and the Rue St. Romain. The first collection of books was destroyed and scattered by the Huguenots, who did

THE INTERIOR.

so much mischief in Rouen in the sixteenth century. A new collection was commenced by François de Harlay, who was archbishop from 1614 to 1651. The Archdeacon Acarie added considerably to this by the gift of all his books in 1632. In 1640 the chapter library was opened to the public, but ceased to exist at the time of the First Revolution.

There are, however, some valuable ancient books still to be seen in the **Treasury**. Among the interesting objects contained in the treasury are a leaden casket in which the heart of Cœur-de-Lion was found in 1838, during some repairs to the cathedral; various tapestries, reliquaries, croziers, vases, montrances, a portrait of Cardinal York the last of the Stuarts; the last Shrine of St. Romain that was used on Ascension Day in the manner already described; and some large music books, in which the notes are of such a size that one book might serve for several choristers at the same time; the notation is in the Gregorian manner—a staff consisting of four lines only.

On the west wall of the transept aisle, close to the door at the bottom of the library staircase, is a doorway leading into a chamber divided longitudinally into two parts by arcading running from north to south. This is lighted by three foliated windows which may be seen from the Cour d'Albane; in the corner between this chamber and the wall of the chapel between the two easternmost buttresses of the nave is another chamber once used as the meeting-place for the chapter, now as a choir vestry.

On the north side of the **North Aisle** of the nave between the buttresses may be seen a series of chapels similar to those on the south side of the church. In the first of these, counting from the east, is the tomb of the second Duke of Normandy, William Longsword, the son of Rollo and Poppa, a count's daughter whom he had seized at Bayeux in his raiding days. This William was murdered in 943. The window of this chapel is, like the one on the opposite side, exceedingly narrow; like all the other windows which light the chapels on this side, it has four lights, and its character is curvilinear Gothic, but the tracery of all the windows is different in detail. In the third bay, counting from the east, the window is short to make room for a door below it; this bay has no altar, but in it may be seen a red marble font. It will be remembered that on the south side the chapel of

St. Stephen under the Butter Tower is opposite to the two westernmost bays of the nave. There is no corresponding chapel on the north side; between the buttresses opposite the second bay there is a small chapel, but there is no entrance into the Tour St. Romain from the church, the lower part of the tower being used as a residence for some of the officials.

Leaving the aisle with its chapels, we will now examine the nave. It will be noticed that the triforium of the four eastern bays differs from that of the seven western; in the latter there is a balustrade with six pointed arches outside the gallery and above it a low arch, whereas in the former the gallery is protected on the outside by arcading which runs up to the string course below the clerestory. The clerestory windows have obtusely pointed heads and geometrical tracery, different in the different windows. Each, however, has four lights.

The pulpit stands on the north side of the nave in the third bay from the east; a partition, which, however, can be moved, runs across the nave from the piers between the fourth and fifth bays counting from the west; to the east of this are chairs for the congregation, the floor of the western part of the nave being left entirely free.

In books published as late as about 1890 a marble screen is described as blocking up the entrance to the choir; this is stated to have been brought by one of the canons from Constantinople. It was erected between 1774 and 1777, but it has now happily disappeared—happily, because it was an incongruous addition to the church, a pseudo-classical barbarism quite out of place among Gothic surroundings. True it is, that there is much classical work in the altars and reredoses of the side chapels, but this does not force itself upon the eye as the choir screen must have done. There are, indeed, in the body of the church scarcely any signs of bad taste, and there is an absence of that tawdry decoration which ruins the effect of many Continental churches.

THE CHOIR.

The usual entrance into the choir is through the south aisle gate. The outer wall is decorated all round, save where screen doorways interrupt it, with arcading, at the

THE INTERIOR.

bottom of which runs a bench table. Above the arcading, arches at the west end open out into the apsidal chapel attached to the east side of the transept, then as the wall at the sixth bay of the choir begins to turn round to the left—for Notre Dame, like most other French churches of any size, has an apsidal ending at the east—we come to the richly carved screen and wrought-iron door of the **Sacristy.** This was erected from a legacy left by Philippe de la Rose, treasurer of the cathedral, who on one occasion played a singular part in the history of the church. After the death of Raoul Roussel in 1452 he was elected archbishop, but the vote in his favour was not unanimous, for a considerable minority of the chapter favoured Richard Olivier, Archdeacon of Eu. The canons appealed to popular judgment and promised to choose that one of the two candidates who should be first carried and placed by the people on the high altar. But public opinion was also divided; some favoured Richard, others Philip. The adherents of the former hastened, the evening before, to the cathedral door, thinking thus to anticipate the supporters of the latter, for they resolved not to allow these to pass through them; but when the door was opened in the morning, and they carried their candidate in triumph to the choir, they beheld Philip, whose friends had passed him in through a window, already mounted on the altar. The archdeacon protested against this trick, but the canons, who had not specified by what way the candidates were to enter the church, felt constrained,

THE CHOIR.

according to their promise, to elect Philip. Richard then set out to Rome to lay the matter before the Pope; but he, in

THE SACRISTY.

order to put an end to the dispute, appointed Cardinal Guillaume d'Estouteville Archbishop of Rouen. Philip's name, however, goes down to history as the judge who pronounced the sentence of rehabilitation in the case of Jeanne d'Arc. On his death he left several sums of money to beautify the cathedral, and his executor, Guillaume Auber, out of this money paid for the construction (1480–1484) of the screen separating the sacristy from the aisle. Within this sacristy, on the left hand, is a beautiful thirteenth century window, and to the east of the sacristy are two similar windows.

Beyond is the **Lady Chapel,** occupying its accustomed place of honour to the due east of the high altar—the first Lady Chapel was built after the great fire about 1214, but by the end of the century it was considered to be far too small, for there seems to have been a considerable outburst of Virgin worship during the thirteenth century, and many Lady Chapels were built or enlarged at this time. Guillaume de Flavacourt, archbishop from 1275–1306, allowed the chapter to take a part of his garden for the extension of the chapel in 1302. The east end of this chapel is apsidal, and contains five windows. The glass dates from 1485; the woodwork and the lead which covers the roof were given by Georges d'Amboise II., and the work was done between 1538 and 1541. The Statue of our Lord was carved by Nicholas Quesnal in 1540, and he received 20 livres for his work. The altar is of seventeenth century date; it is of carved wood and was gilded in 1825.

But it is not this gilded altar that will attract the attention of the visitor, but the elaborate **monuments** on either side of the chapel. The first tomb on the north side, which is often overlooked, beautiful though it is, on account of the great size of its neighbours, is that of Pierre de Brézé, Lord of Varenne and Count of Maulevrier; he lived in the fifteenth century, was the favourite and Prime Minister of Charles VII., and took an active part in the conquest of Normandy in 1449, was the first to enter Rouen, and was granted the high-sounding title of Grand Seneschal of Normandy. He was the first to fall in the battle of Montlhéry on July 16th, 1465. His body was brought a few days later to the cathedral and buried with all honour. His monument was erected in 1488 by his son, Jacques de Brézé, who succeeded him in his high office. His wife was buried by his side, and formerly their statues lay side by side on the tomb, but they were taken away by an order of the chapter in 1769 which directed the removal of all dilapidated statues from the church. Just to the east of this stands the

THE LADY CHAPEL FROM THE EAST.

more pretentious monument of Louis de Brézé, grandson of Pierre, Grand Seneschal of Normandy. He died on July 20th,

MONUMENTS OF PIERRE AND LOUIS DE BRÉZÉ.

1531, and this monument was raised to his memory by his wife, Diana of Poitiers. On the black marble sarcophagus lies the naked body of Louis, carved in white marble, just as he may well have appeared in death; kneeling at his head Diana weeps over him, and at his feet stands Mary with the child Jesus in her arms, looking on unconcernedly; above may be seen a white marble statue of the duke as he appeared in life, armed in full armour on his mail-clad horse. There is a touching inscription in which his widow, after asserting her fidelity to him during his lifetime, professes that her fidelity to his memory shall continue after his death. If she had lived but eight years after her husband she might have kept her word, for it was in the ninth year of her widowhood that she became the mistress of Henry II. This monument is said to be the joint work of Jean Cousin and Jean Goujon.

On the opposite side is the more beautiful monument erected in memory of **Cardinal Georges d'Amboise.** He has been so often mentioned in connection with the cathedral that this will be a fitting place to tell something of the story of this great ecclesiastic and statesman. Born in 1460, he became Bishop of Montauban when only fourteen years of age, and Louis XI. made him one of his almoners. He afterwards espoused the cause of the Duke of Orleans and was imprisoned for this; but when the duke was restored to the king's favour he became archbishop, first of Narbonne, then of Rouen. The manner of his election to the latter post will be told presently. Under the duke he did much for Normandy, ridding it of bandits and saving the people from the tyranny of the nobles. When the duke ascended the throne as Louis XII. Georges d'Amboise became his Prime Minister and also a cardinal. His influence was good; his voice was always raised on the side of justice and of mercy; he was active in reforming the Church, and was noted for his deeds of charity, especially at the time of the plague in 1504. He has sometimes been called the French Wolsey because, like the English cardinal, he was ambitious and aimed at the Papacy, and, like him, was on two occasions disappointed; but to his credit be it told, that when he might have used French troops to overawe the College and secure his election, he refused to use force. He died at Lyons in 1510.

The story of his election is as follows: On July 19th, 1493,

THE INTERIOR. 53

the archiepiscopal ring still remained on the dead finger of Robert de Croixmare, the late archbishop. The body, in all its ecclesiastical vestments, was brought into the cathedral, and that

MONUMENT OF THE TWO CARDINALS D'AMBOISE.

same night was carried, as the custom was, to the neighbouring abbey church of St. Ouen, there to rest till the next morning, while the monks of St. Ouen kept vigil by it. On the next day it was carried past the abbey of St. Amand, of which a few remains may still be seen in the Rue St. Amand, and the abbess, according to ancient custom, removed the ring from his finger to keep until his successor should come to claim it. The chapter sent word to the king, Charles VIII., that they were proceeding to elect an archbishop. Charles sent back answer that he neither admitted nor denied their right to elect, and hinted that it was his wish that the friend of his good friend the Duke of Orleans should be chosen. The duke also expressed his wishes on the subject. This interference with their free choice somewhat irritated the canons, and they would give no definite undertaking to elect the royal nominee. Great was the excitement in the city as August 21st, the day of the election, drew nigh. The church was densely packed, for all desired to know as soon as possible the result of the election. The canons retired to the chapter-house, the doors were shut, the oath to vote according to their conscience was administered to all the electors. An address on the importance of their choice was given; the canons knelt on the floor, sang the "*Veni creator spiritus*," and prayed for divine guidance. Then, suddenly, all leapt to their feet at once and cried aloud "Georges d'Amboise shall be archbishop." The news was soon noised abroad, and next day the archbishop-elect walked barefoot to the abbey of St. Amand to receive the ring which the abbess gave him with the accustomed words, "Messire, je le donne à vous vivant, vous me le

REMAINS OF THE ABBEY OF ST. AMAND.

rendrez mort." Then returning to Notre Dame he took the oaths and was enthroned as archbishop and blessed his flock. Well in after years he kept his oath, and cathedral and city alike had reason to bless the day when the vote of the chapter was given to Georges d'Amboise. And here on his costly tomb, erected by his nephew and successor Georges d'Amboise II. (1510-1556), carved by Roullant Le Roux, he kneels in stone. Seven years did the carvers work at this gorgeous tomb, and finished it in 1525. The face of the statue is evidently a good likeness; the square head, deep brow, and firm mouth are such as we can well imagine belonged to the firm administrator who left his impress more strongly marked on the cathedral and city than any one before or after him.

> "Pastor eram cleri, populi pater, aurea sese
> Lilia[1] subdebant quercus[2] et ipsa mihi.
> Mortuus en jaceo morte extinguuntur honores
> At virtus mortis nescia morte viret."

is the proud inscription on the tomb.

The six statues of the face on the monument represent Faith, Charity, Prudence, Temperance, Courage, Justice. In the central panel behind the cardinal is carved his patron saint St. George slaying the dragon, and in the niches on either side we see, beginning from the left, a bishop, the Virgin and Child, John the Baptist, St. Romain and Gargouille, a man clothed in a garment of haircloth, and an archbishop giving his blessing. Above the canopy are nineteen figures representing the apostles and other saints.

The second statue that kneels upon the tomb behind the other represents Georges d'Amboise II. It was placed here after his death. The head of this statue was sculptured by Jean Gougon. The statues of these great prelates remain there to this day, but in 1793 the grave was opened, the dust of the archbishops cast away, and their lead coffins melted and cast into bullets.

Though these archbishops have the most striking memorials, yet they are not the only prelates that lie buried in the Lady Chapel. Here, too, were laid the remains of previous occupiers of the archbishop's throne, Eude Rigaud 1275, Guillaume de Flavacourt 1306, Raoul Roussel 1452, and Robert de Croixmare 1493.

[1] Emblems of the French king. [2] Emblems of the Pope Rovère.

In the north-east wall of the cathedral, to the left of the entrance to the Lady Chapel, beneath a round-headed arch behind the thirteenth century arcading, is the monument of Archbishop Maurice, 1235. A little further to the left is the chapel of St. Peter and St. Paul; enclosed within the wall are the remains of Matilda, wife of Henry V. of Germany.

Other illustrious dead found a resting-place within the cathedral walls; the heart of the lion-hearted King of England once lay beneath the sanctuary floor, and the body of his brother Henry, who died in 1183, and that of John Duke of Bedford, regent of English France in the fifteenth century, were also buried here.

TOMB OF ARCHBISHOP MAURICE.

To return once again to the architectural features of the building. The choir proper is divided from its encircling aisle and ambulatory by an arcading of fourteen circular pillars with lofty capitals and circular abaci. The carving on the two western capitals differs somewhat from that on the others; the form may be seen in the illustrations. The arches are all pointed; the five at the east are stilted, for here the pillars are set more closely together. The triforium gallery runs behind an arcading of lancet-headed arches. The clerestory windows are of ample size, their heads more pointed than those of the nave clerestory windows; those on the south and north have each four lights, while those round the east end have but three.

The **Choir Stalls** were erected largely at the cost of

THE CHOIR FROM THE SOUTH AISLE OF THE NAVE.

Guillaume d'Estouteville between the years 1457 and 1469. The design is due to Philippe Viart, "Maistre Huchier" of Rouen, who employed sundry Flemish carvers in wood to execute them, as well as French carpenters, whose names can be read in the chapter accounts. There are now eighty-six stalls, and though they have been much mutilated and two have disappeared altogether, the misereres are in many instances perfect. Some of these were no doubt copied from the carvings on the walls outside, and many of them represent men and women occupied in their every-day businesses — the wool-comber, the cobbler, the barber and surgeon, the schoolmaster, the carver, the mason, the blacksmith, the shepherd, the gardener, the fisherman, the chemist, and the housemaid. Besides all these there are various grotesque monsters, suggested possibly by the masked figures that took part in the mediæval revels. The canopies which probably rose over the rear rank of the stalls have perished, and iron railings now separate the choir and sanctuary from the aisles and ambulatory.

THE ABBEY CHURCH OF ST. OUEN

ST. OUEN FROM THE NORTH-WEST.

THE ABBEY CHURCH OF ST. OUEN.

CHAPTER I.

HISTORY OF THE BUILDING.

THE church of St. Ouen which we see to-day is one that has called forth the admiration of many competent judges. The aged verger tells all English visitors that the greatest of all Englishmen whom he has known, Mr. John Ruskin, often declared it in his hearing to be the most perfect monument of pure Gothic in the world; and Fergusson, in his *History of Architecture*, writes of it in the following enthusiastic terms:—
"The Church of St. Ouen at Rouen is beyond comparison the most beautiful and perfect of the abbey edifices of France. . . . Except that of Limoges, the choir is almost the only perfect building of its age, and being nearly contemporaneous with the choir at Cologne (1276–1312), affords a means of comparison between the two styles of Germany and France at that age, entirely to the advantage of the French example, which, though very much smaller, avoids all the more glaring faults of the other. Nothing, indeed, can exceed the beauty of proportion of this most elegant church; and except that it wants the depth and earnestness of the earlier examples, it may be considered the most beautiful thing of its kind in Europe. The proportion, too, of the nave, transepts, and choir to one another is remarkably happy, and affords a most striking contrast to the imperfect proportions of Cologne. Its three towers, also, would have formed a perfect group as originally

designed; but the central one was not completed till so late that its details have lost the aspiring character of the building on which it stands, and the western spires, as rebuilt within the last few years, are incongruous and inappropriate; whereas had the original design been carried out according to the drawings which still exist, it would have been one of the most beautiful façades known anywhere. The diagonal position of the towers met most happily the difficulty of giving breadth to the façade without placing them beyond the line of the aisles, as is done in the Cathedral of Rouen, and at the same time gave a variety to the perspective which must have had the most pleasing effect. Had this idea occurred earlier, few western towers would have been placed otherwise; but the invention came too late, and within the last few years we have seen all traces of the arrangement ruthlessly obliterated."

But this magnificent church is not the first that occupied this site; in fact, several churches have stood upon it, and have passed away leaving not a trace behind. We may regret this; still, as some compensation, we may note the fact that owing to the entire destruction of previous buildings we have now a perfect example of a large church built for the most part within a very short time, showing great unity of design and general character.

There is a legend that the earliest church on the site of St. Ouen was founded about the year 400; but the earliest authentic evidence existing is that of a monk, Fredegonde, who tells us of the foundation of a church dedicated to the apostles Peter and Paul by Hlothair, though some imagine that his work was only the rebuilding of a more ancient structure; be this as it may, this church, after the translation to it, a few years after his death, of the remains of St. Ouen, Archbishop of Rouen, who died in 686, received the name it now bears. This church was destroyed by the Norse Vikings when they first sailed up the Seine as far as Rouen in 841; but after their leader, Hrolf the Ganger or Walker, so called, according to tradition, because on account of his gigantic size he could find no horse large and strong enough to carry him, had become the first recognised Duke of Normandy, and had embraced the Christian faith, he rebuilt the ruined church. In all probability the earlier church was in great measure a wooden structure, and so had been easily destroyed.

HISTORY OF THE BUILDING.

It may assist the reader to understand the details of the early history of this church, if a list is given of the Norman dukes whose names will be mentioned in connection with it. Hrolf, whose name now appears on his statue to the south side of the church of St. Ouen, and on his tomb in Notre Dame as Rollon, died in 931, and was succeeded by William Longsword, who was murdered in 943; to him succeeded Richard I., surnamed the "Fearless," who in 996 was succeeded by Richard II. or the "Good," who dying in 1026 left his dukedom to his son Richard III., who died two years afterwards and was succeeded by Robert, surnamed the Magnificent and also the Devil, the father of that great duke known in English history as William the Conqueror, who obtained the Norman coronet in 1035, and the English crown in 1066, and died in 1087.

The foundation of a new church dedicated to St. Ouen was, as stated above, laid by Rollo, and the work of building it was carried on by Richard I. and Richard II., but the abbot Nicholas, son of Richard III., dissatisfied with its dimensions and characters, had it demolished and laid the foundation-stone of a new church and the domestic buildings of the abbey about 1045. This new church was, of course, of stone, and must have been built in what we should call in England the Early Norman style. The workmanship was doubtless rude, the walls, piers, and round-headed arches massive, though probably, as it was only finished some eighty years later, when Guillaume I. was abbot, and as architecture had made great strides during this period, we may well imagine that some greater refinement and more richly decorated work marked some parts of the building. The completed church was dedicated on October 26th, 1126, by Godfrey, Archbishop of Rouen.

At the time of its erection the abbey of St. Ouen was outside the city walls, but a few years later the boundaries were extended, so that it was comprised within the circuit of the new walls. This church was not destined long to stand in its completed state, for ten years after its dedication it was destroyed by fire. It was then rebuilt, the empress Matilda and Richard Cœur de Lion helping in the work, but in 1248 it once again fell a prey to the same enemy. The first stone of the church, we now see, was laid on the 25th May 1318 by the abbot Jean Roussel, otherwise called Marc d'Argent. Hence it appears that it is certainly the fifth, possibly the sixth church that has occupied the same site.

Of the earlier churches nothing remains save the little fragment known as the Tour aux Clercs, which is probably part of the church built by Nicholas and his successors in the twelfth century. The work went briskly on in the days of Marc d'Argent. So accurate were the accounts kept, that we are told that during twenty-one years the abbot spent 63,936 livres and 5 sous on the work. The monks worked at the building with the ordinary masons, and during those twenty-one years the choir, most of the chapels that surround it, and part of the transept were completed. This brings us to the year 1339. Our third Edward was now sitting on the English throne, and had set up his extravagant claim to the French crown. The next year saw the first outbreak of hostilities between France and England known as the "hundred years' war." The disturbed condition of the country owing to this, led to an interruption in church building operations, but from 1378 to 1398 we find the work again prospering under Jean de Bayeaux. By this time Edward III. and his son the Black Prince were both in their graves, and Richard II., the new king, had troubles enough at home to prevent him from interfering with France. From 1411 to 1421 another Jean de Bayeaux, son of the one just mentioned, was master-builder. In 1413 Henry V. ascended the English throne, and he was not slow to revive the old claim made by his great-grandfather. War broke out in 1415; and during this, Normandy greatly suffered. In 1417 Henry landed, and soon reduced Falaise, Evreux, and Caen, and then laid siege to Rouen. The city offered a strenuous resistance to his arms. All the citizens were called upon to give money to aid in the preparations for defending the city; but so eager were the monks to advance the building of their abbey, that they refused to contribute to the defence, preferring to spend their money on the walls of the church rather than on military works. Unpatriotic no doubt they were considered by the people of Rouen, but they had their reward, for after the town had been taken, and the English kings were again for a time masters of the duchy which their ancestors had held, Alexander de Berneval, who was architect from

HISTORY OF THE BUILDING. 65

1422-1441, carried on the work with the full sanction of the English. This Berneval built the chapel of SS. Peter and

NORTH TRANSEPT.

Paul, and designed and completed the circular window in the south transept; and according to a legend still very generally believed, in a fit of jealousy killed a pupil, who had designed the corresponding window in the north transept, because it was considered superior to his own in beauty, and was hung for the crime in 1441; but in consideration of the work he had done for the abbey, he was buried within its walls by the monks, and his tomb may be seen to this day. Incised on the wall of a chapel on the north side of the choir are two figures, one that of Alexander de Berneval, for the following inscription identifies it:—

> Ci gist Alexandre de Berneval
> Maistre des Oeubres de Machonnerie
> du Roy notre sire, du Baillage de Rouen
> et de ceste Eglise, que trespassa l'an de
> grace mil ccccxl le V jour de Janbier
> Priés Dieu pour l'ame de ly.

The other, which has no inscription, is generally taken to be his pupil, whose body was interred, so it is said, by the side of his master and murderer. In confirmation of this legend is shown a painted window in a chapel further to the east, which is said to represent the execution of Berneval; certain it is that there is the figure of a man hanging on a gallows. But the truth of this story is doubtful; it seems unlikely that the abbot would ever have allowed a murderer who had been publicly executed to be buried within the walls of the abbey church; and it is said by some authorities that the figure taken for the pupil and victim is really that of Colin Berneval, his son, who succeeded his father as architect. Nothing, moreover, about his crime or its punishment is said in the inscription just quoted.

Colin Berneval commenced the central tower, but the upper part was not finished till the end of the fifteenth century, when it was completed by Jacques Theroulde in the days of the abbot Antoine Bohier (1490-1515). The same abbot built the Portail des Marmosets, as the door of the south transept is called, and lengthened the nave westward; his successor added yet four more bays, and built the western façade and the bases of the western towers. This end of the church, however, was never entirely completed; the western towers, by the middle of the sixteenth century, had reached the height of

HISTORY OF THE BUILDING. 67

about 150 feet. These, as already mentioned, were placed diagonally, so that the great western doorway was set as it were in a recess. It was intended to finish the towers with octagonal crowns similar to that of the central tower, but this was never done; and when the Government had in the nineteenth century classed the church of St. Ouen among the number of national monuments, it was resolved, in the reign of Louis Philippe, to complete the western façade. A million and a half francs were

WEST FRONT.

voted for this purpose on June 22nd, 1845. The preparation of a design was intrusted to the official architect of the department, M. Grégoire, and to him is due the cold and formal west front as we see it at the present time. Loaded though it is with carving, large though these western porches are, yet it does not arrest the attention, and bears no comparison in beauty to the west front of the cathedral. The whole of the old west front was pulled down, together with the diagonal towers; and that peculiar feature which Fergusson thinks such a happy thought of Cibo's architect, and which he says would probably have become a favourite arrangement had there been any more large churches built in mediæval times, was utterly destroyed. For what conceivable reason this destruction was proposed and actually carried out, we cannot say; probably it was due to the utterly vitiated taste of the middle of the nineteenth century, and although probably one of the most glaring instances of the mischief done under the name of restoration, it was by no means the only one. At the same time, houses which clustered along the south side of the nave were swept away, so that an uninterrupted view of this side of the building can be obtained. In fact, in this respect St. Ouen is singularly fortunate among continental churches; so many of them are so closely blocked in that their exteriors can only be seen piecemeal if at all. In many instances it may be that a general view would not be pleasing; but St. Ouen owes so much of its claim upon our admiration to its exquisite proportions, that we may be doubly grateful for the fact that the whole can be so well seen. One can only wish that the restorers had seen their way not only to destroy the old houses on the south, but to also sweep away the exceedingly ugly building abutting upon the north transept, now the Hotel de Ville. Part of this building formed the monks' dormitory, and was erected in the latter part of the eighteenth century, when the monastic body, having more money than they knew what to do with, resolved to rebuild their domestic buildings. This work was in progress when the Revolution interrupted it, and the monks, who numbered only twelve, were expelled from their abbey,[1] and in 1803, when things had become more settled, the new building was taken possession of by the civil authorities to be used as a town hall. The sixteenth century abbots' house was pulled down in 1816, and other Gothic remains of the old abbey were likewise swept away, and between 1826 and 1829 the Hotel de Ville was enlarged to its present dimensions. The abbey church, after the dissolution of the monastery, became simply a parish church, as did many of the abbey churches in England.

This church has suffered much from ill-treatment at various

[1] The last abbot was Etienne Charles de Lomenie de Brienne. A warrant was issued for his arrest in 1794, but he was found dead in his bed when the officers came to take him.

times. The Huguenots sacked it in 1562; at the time of the Revolution it was converted into a museum, and even for a time blacksmiths' forges were erected and arms were forged within its walls; the smoke from the fires has darkened the walls of the interior. But despite all its misfortunes, even including the greatest of all, its restoration, it is still an object of beauty, and its beauty is of a kind that grows upon one the longer one looks at it.

The abbey, too, has been connected with many events in history which could be told did space allow. For it was one of the most important of the monastic bodies in Normandy, holding lands in many parts of the Province.

Two events, however, took place within the abbey precincts of such interest to English people that they must be briefly sketched here. On a scaffolding erected in the open space that surrounded the unfinished nave, on the Thursday after Pentecost in 1431, might be seen a priestly gang and an innocent girl. For on one side sat my Lord Cardinal of Winchester with his supporting clerics, Pierre Cauchon, Bishop of Beauvais among them, and fronting them stood Jeanne d'Arc.[1] She had been brought hither to publicly abjure her sins, to confess that the voices she had heard were but delusions of her brain or whisperings of the evil spirit, that she had had no divine commission to bring about the coronation of the king at Rheims. Worn out by the long ceremony, terrified by the threats of immediate burning if she did not abjure, she at last declared that she submitted to the Church. But her submission did her no good. Discovered in a fresh crime, that of resuming the male attire she had adopted as a safeguard and now wore again for the same reason, she was condemned to perish at the stake in the Vieux Marché, and there on May 30th she was slowly burnt to death. The king whom she had placed upon the throne made no effort to save her; no Privilege de la Fierte de St. Romain was exercised on her behalf. The people wept around her, but did not interfere. She perished in the flames, and her ashes were collected and thrown into the Seine. But in the year 1456 a " Procès de Rehabilitation " was begun, and on the 7th

---

[1] It is doubtful which is the correct way of spelling her name. I here adopt that which is prevalent in Modern Rouen.—T. P.

day of July, in accordance with a decree passed in the archbishop's palace on the spot where she had died, and also in the cemetery of St. Ouen where she had made her abjuration, her innocence was publicly proclaimed and her honour vindicated.

THE CHURCH FROM THE NORTH-EAST.

CHAPTER II.

THE EXTERIOR.

THE whole of the exterior of this church can be well seen. Wide open spaces extend on every side of it; no building save the Hotel de Ville, which, as stated in the last chapter, was once part of the domestic buildings of the abbey, approaches it, and this is a long narrow building whose south end almost joins the north transept, but does not hide any considerable part of the church.

We will begin our examination at the north-west angle of the transept, just in front of the south end of the western face of the Hotel de Ville. This spot is shown in the general view from the north-west (see illustration, p. 60). It will be seen that the nave consists of nine bays marked by tall and substantial buttresses whose outer faces project beyond the aisles and rise vertically from the ground. These are surmounted by crocketed pinnacles, each crowned with a statue. It was necessary to make these buttresses strong, because they have to withstand the thrust of the lofty vaulting transmitted to them by flying buttresses passing over the roof of the nave aisle and at a considerable distance above it. The pier buttresses do not increase to the extent that our buttresses often do as they near the ground, for, though built in several stages, each offset projects but slightly; hence the church gains in apparent height. In the angle between the transept aisle and north choir aisle is a rectangular chamber, and beyond this under the windows of the aisle runs a long low building whose bays are narrower than those of the nave. This is used for the choristers.

We next come to the **North-West Tower**; the lowest stage of this rises to the level of the walls of the aisles and is square, the next stage rising nearly to the same level as the ridge of the nave roof is octagonal; above this is another octagonal stage with unglazed openings in every face, and above this an octagonal spire with crockets along each edge. The whole is

THE SOUTH SIDE.

very highly decorated. In the lowest stage are two portals, recessed and surmounted by traceried gables. One of these portals opens to the north, one to the west; next we come to the central west portal. The doorway beneath the tympanum is

THE EXTERIOR.   75

double, with a stone division between the two doors; these are of the same height as the lateral doors, but the double opening is wider, and the door is more deeply recessed. A richly carved and lofty gable with open tracery rises above this portal and partly conceals the west window of the nave behind it. All the details may be better understood by the reader by examining the illustration (p. 67) than by any elaborate verbal description.

The **South-West Tower** corresponds exactly to the north-west one; and as we pass along the south side of the nave, we see no fresh features until we come to the south transept, save that on this side there are no buildings outside the aisles. A small door opens into the fifth bay from the west, and to the east of this we pass through a gate into the gardens of the Hotel de Ville, which surround the east end of the church. These are beautifully kept; the grass is closely cut and well watered, and must on no account be trodden on. The writer incurred the anger of one of the gendarmes because, when taking a photograph to illustrate this book (that on p. 74), one leg of his camera trespassed on the forbidden ground. Here stands a modern statue of Rollo, the first Duke of Normandy.

Standing to the south of the "Portail des Marmosets," as the **South Transept** doorway is called, on account of some figures of these animals which are carved upon it, one notices at once a great difference between this entrance and the Portail de Calende, which occupies the corresponding position in the cathedral. There we saw a deeply recessed doorway like the entrance to a cavern. Here we have an archway in an outer wall forming a distinct porch, such as we frequently meet with in English churches, with side walls, and within it a vaulted roof between the outer walls and the doorway, which is double. The portal is one of great beauty and lightness; the foliated cusps beneath the outer archway are especially light. It seems almost impossible that they could long resist the effects of wind and rain; indeed, from the sharpness of the carving, one is tempted to think that they have been repaired at no very distant date. The carving of the tympanum in three tiers is very lovely. It represents the death and assumption of the Virgin. This carving is placed so that it can be well seen, and has been protected by its position within the outer porch; but as the only light it receives is from the front, the details are not easy to photograph.

76   THE ABBEY CHURCH OF ST. OUEN.

Above the porch may be seen two windows which light a room used as the library of the church; above this, at some distance behind it, is the magnificent rose window of the elder Berneval,

SOUTH TRANSEPT.

a beautiful example of Flamboyant tracery; above this, in a series of niches at the base of the transept gable, are six statues, representing respectively Clothair I., Richard I., Richard II.,

PORTAIL DES MARMOSETS.

the Empress Matilda, Philippe le Loney and his wife, all benefactors of the abbey, and at the summit of the gable is a statue of St. Ouen, to whom the church is dedicated. To the east of the porch is a low chamber lit by five windows with curvilinear tracery, four looking towards the south and one towards the east.

Passing on, we see the chapels of the **Chevet,** which entirely surround the choir; these are eleven in number. The central one, facing the east, is naturally the Lady Chapel; these have pyramidal roofs, as will be seen from the illustration, p. 80. It will have been noticed that side chapels only exist round the eastern arm of the building; there are none along the sides of the nave. The greater width of the choir necessitates a different system of external buttressing from that adopted in the nave. The flying buttresses are arranged in two tiers one above the other, and each buttress is double arched, the inner buttresses spanning the width of the arches and abutting against pinnacles rising from the walls of the aisles; the outer springing across the roofs of the chapels and abutting against the vertical buttresses running up against the outer walls of the chapels. These vertical buttresses are loaded with tall pinnacles, each one bearing a statue at its summit. It will not be necessary to enter into any detailed description of the appearance of this system of flying buttresses, as the illustration on p. 81, reproduced from a photograph taken from the roof of the transept, shows the arrangement clearly. There is a passage within a pierced parapet running all round the roof of the church. This can be reached by a staircase from the south transept; a fee of two francs is charged for permission to climb to the roof, but the money is well expended; for from this passage the beautiful central tower is best seen, and in addition to this a magnificent view of the city is obtained. It will be noticed that the parapet of the walls of the nave is not exactly in a straight line. Mr. Ruskin severely criticises the flying buttresses that run from the octagonal crown of the tower to the turrets that spring from the corners of the main tower below. On page 38 of the *Seven Lamps* he thus writes: " In later Gothic the pinnacle becomes gradually a decorative member, and was used in all places merely for its beauty. There is no objection to this . . . . but also the buttress became a decorative member; and was used,

80   THE ABBEY CHURCH OF ST. OUEN.

first, where it was not wanted, and, secondly, in forms in which

PART OF THE CHEVET.

it could be of no use, becoming a mere tie, not between the

pier and wall, but between the pier and the top of the decorative pinnacle, thus attaching itself to the very point where

FLYING BUTTRESSES OF THE CHOIR.

its thrust, if it made any, could not be resisted. The most flagrant instance of this barbarism that I remember is the lantern of St. Ouen at Rouen, where the pierced buttress, having an ogee curve, looks about as much calculated to bear a thrust as a switch of willow; and the pinnacles, huge and richly decorated, have evidently no work to do whatever but stand round the central tower, like four idle servants as they are—heraldic supporters, that central tower being merely a hollow crown, which needs no more buttressing than a basket does." That there is some truth in this one cannot deny, but the buttresses do not, as the reader of the passage might imagine, join the top of the pinnacles, but abut against their sides, somewhat, indeed, above their middle points; but that they are ornamental only can be easily seen. Mr. Ruskin goes on to say that the whole tower "is one of the basest pieces of Gothic in Europe, its Flamboyant traceries being of the most degraded forms; and its entire plan and decoration resembling and deserving little more credit than the burnt sugar ornaments of elaborate confectionery." In Appendix II. he makes some very uncomplimentary remarks about the whole church of St. Ouen. Its nave, he says, is a base imitation of an early Gothic arrangement; the niches on the piers barbarisms, the south porch extravagant and almost grotesque. In fact, he concludes by saying that "there is nothing truly fine in the church but the choir, the light triforium and the tall clerestory, the circle of eastern chapels, the details of sculpture, and the general lightness of proportion." All this is singularly at variance with the opinion expressed to the verger and quoted by him, that the church is "le plus beau monument de pure gothique dans tout le monde," but Mr. Ruskin had a habit of contradicting himself, or at anyrate of changing his opinions, so that the visitor to the abbey church need not be ashamed if he finds much in it to admire. Fergusson's pronouncement on the central tower is: "Had the western tower been completed in the same character in accordance with the original design, the towers of this church would probably be unrivalled. Even alone, the lantern is a very noble architectural feature and appropriate to its position, though some of the details mark the lateness of the age in which it was erected."

Passing round the chevet we cannot help being struck by the light and simple tracery of the windows, pure geometrical in character, but we also regret that the same forms have been so often repeated

THE EXTERIOR. 83

There are a few features to be noticed on the north side of the choir in which it differs from the south. First, the manner in which the end of the **North Transept** is supported by flying buttresses. The reason for their insertion is not apparent; they do not seem to be necessitated by the

TOUR AUX CLERCS.

thrust of the vault; it may be that some subsidence of the foundation threatened to give trouble. Another most interesting feature is the two-staged building known as the **Tour aux Clercs.** This stands at the north-east angle of the transept, and is in all probability the remains of an apsidal chapel attached to the transept of the church commenced by the abbot Nicholas in the year 1046, which was burnt in 1136. The style of architecture indicates that it was built in the eleventh century. On the eastern face there is a doorway with a flat arched top, above this a round-headed window, and at a considerably higher level, another similar window with shafts set in its jambs. The tower, which is semicircular in plan, is surrounded by five string courses and is crowned with a pierced parapet in continuation of that which runs round the top of the wall of the chapels surrounding the choir, which is at the same level

We have now made a complete circuit of the church, from the south-west to the south-east corner of the Hotel de Ville, and we must have been struck by the simplicity and uniformity of its plan, as well as by the lavish ornamentation expended on it. It would need much patience to count the pinnacles that rise from wall and buttress, and when we notice the crockets which decorate every edge of these and the statues that stand on every pinnacle, we may realise the enormous amount of work that went to the building of this great church, for vast indeed it is in size. It slightly exceeds in length and breadth Salisbury Cathedral, which is, I believe, considered about seventh in size among our English cathedral and abbey churches, and in height it exceeds Westminster, which has the loftiest nave of any church in England. It is said that its windows number 135, not counting the three large roses; and as the principal windows are all of large size, extending from buttress to buttress, it can well be imagined how vast a flood of light is let in. These windows all contain painted glass. That in the choir and its chapel dates chiefly from the fourteenth century, while that in the nave windows is for the most part due to the fifteenth century. It would seem that as the tracery of the windows was completed the painted glass was put in.

There is one aspect under which the exterior may be viewed which no visitor, if the opportunity occurs, should miss. If, during his stay in Rouen, there should chance to be a clear moonlight night, he should take his stand in the street to the south of the nave, and gaze on the vast pile before him. He will see the lower part of the building illuminated by the electric light of the street lamps, but the central tower, owing to its great height, will receive scarcely any light from these, and will be lit almost entirely by the moonlight alone, and rise white and ghost-like against the sky.

THE NAVE.

CHAPTER III.

THE INTERIOR.

In order to obtain the most striking first impression of the interior of the church of St. Ouen, it is well to enter it by one of the western doors and to take one's stand beneath the organ, which here, as at Notre Dame, is placed in a gallery at the west end over the great central doorway. It is a glorious sight that meets the eye: the vista before one is as long as that in many of our most magnificent cathedral churches, and is unbroken by any screen dividing choir from nave, and the lofty roof is hung some hundred feet above one's head higher than any vault we have in England. The height, great as it is, is increased in appearance by the fact that the main vaulting shafts rise unbroken from the pavement to their capitals above the level of the sills of the clerestory windows, from which spring the diagonal and transverse ribs of the roof. The central ridge of the vaulting is practically unbroken from end to end, for the central tower does not open, as at Notre Dame, to the crossing; and at the east end three tiers of windows, those of the Lady Chapel, are seen through the arcading that encircles the choir, while above are the large windows over the triforium gallery, and above them the three vast windows of the apsidal clerestory. We in England are accustomed, as a rule, to one large flat east window; but grand as the effect of this may be, yet it will generally be allowed that the apsidal ending is more beautiful. In most, if not all of our English churches, we have well-marked horizontal lines: first the row of capitals of the nave piers, then often a string course running along above the crowns of the arches, unbroken from end to end of the nave, and the triforium gallery similarly divided from the clerestory, all which horizontal lines tend to lower the apparent height of the already low vaulting of the roof; but in the church of St. Ouen, as we gaze on the interior from the west end, we find it marked by a profusion of vertical lines giving the appearance of increased height. Here it may be mentioned that the ratio of height to breadth is about three to one, differing but little from the ratio at Westminster, and exceeding that of all other English churches, where in some cases, as at York, Lincoln, Peterborough, Wells, Exeter, and Lichfield, it falls as low as about two to one. No gloomy shadows hang about the lofty vault, for the great clerestory windows flood the upper part with light while the windows of the aisles light the lower part, so that a most even effect is produced.

It will be well to examine the system of **vaulting** from this point of view. It is quadripartite, that is to say, from each pair of main vaulting shafts spring transverse ribs dividing the roof into compartments rectangular in plan, whose breadths from north to south are about 34 feet, and length from east to west about 20 feet. From the four capitals of the main vaulting shafts, at the corner of each of the compartments, other vaulting ribs spring diagonally, dividing each compartment into four spaces triangular in plan. But something more must also be noticed—the ribs which run round the clerestory openings, which may be called longitudinal ribs, do not spring from the same level as the transverse and diagonal ribs, but from a higher level. The shafts that support the longitudinal ribs rise from the floor and run up in a vertical line some feet above the capitals of the main vaulting shafts. There is a twofold advantage in this. First, it allows the clerestory windows to be wider; in fact, there is no solid wall space between the clerestory windows and the shafts; and secondly, it narrows the space on which the thrust of the vault presses, and therefore makes it more easy to resist the thrust by the external flying buttresses. It is said by some that the plan of making the longitudinal ribs spring from a higher level than the transverse and diagonal ones was adopted simply for the former reason; but since it is found in buildings in which the clerestory windows do not occupy the whole space of the wall, it is evident that it was adopted as a means of facilitating the resistance of the thrust by the flying buttress resting against the wall at the higher level. But when it had been

THE INTERIOR.

once adopted for this purpose it gave the opportunity for enlarging the windows which the later Gothic architects were only too ready to avail themselves of, in order to display their painted glass. By reference to the illustration on p. 93 it will be seen that the outer walls of St. Ouen are little else than a sheet of glass, set, as it were, in a stone framework, slender indeed as seen from the inside, so slender that it could not possibly support the vault of heavy stone had it not been for the buttresses without.

The whole secret of this marvellous mechanical contrivance may be seen by reference to the illustration given in the last chapter, p. 81. The weight of the vault tends to push out the walls, but by the contrivance of the vaulting ribs the pressure is brought to bear upon points situated between the heads of the clerestory windows, and the flying buttresses act like the wooden props that we sometimes see used to shore up the walls of a house which are falling outwards, the other ends resting on the standing buttresses, which from their weight, increased by the pinnacles that stand upon them, are sufficiently strong to keep the walls from spreading, so that practically the vaulting has not a narrow base of some 35 feet, the distance between the vaulting shafts which one sees resting on the floor of the church, but rests upon a space about 100 feet wide in the nave and about 135 feet wide in the choir, for these are approximately the distances between the exterior faces of the buttresses in the nave and choir respectively. It is by their perfect system of wide exterior buttressing that the French Gothic architects were enabled to support their great stone vaults at such a height above the ground; the higher the vault the broader necessarily must be their base upon the ground. From what has been said it will be seen that in the case of the church of St. Ouen this width in the nave is about equal to the height of the vault, and in the choir exceeds it.[1] The same principle may be seen employed in the cathedral church of Notre Dame, but as the difficulty that confronted the builders was greater in the case of the church of St. Ouen, the discussion of the system has been deferred to the present place. The builders of English churches did not raise their roofs so high as the

[1] For more detailed discussion of this point, the reader is referred to Moore's *Gothic Architecture*, Chap. II.

French, hence there was less need of buttressing; and in many of our cathedrals no flying buttresses are to be met with, though sometimes what are practically flying buttresses are

SOUTH AISLE.

concealed beneath the roof of the triforium; in other cases the roofs are not stone vaults at all but are formed of wood, and in these the thrust can be counteracted by tie beams above the ceilings.

THE INTERIOR.

To return, however, to a description of the church of St. Ouen. The piers of the **nave** arcading have no general capitals,

THE WEST END OF THE NAVE.

only the slender inner shaft, from which springs the central moulding of the arch, is thus provided; but every pier has projecting brackets, intended to support statues, and canopies above them, and if we pass through the arcading into the aisles we shall notice a very ugly feature—square shafts used to strengthen the piers which run up through the vaulting of the

VIEW FROM NORTH AISLE OF NAVE, LOOKING INTO THE CHOIR.

aisles. On the south side of the nave, attached to the first pier, is a holy water stoup of black marble veined with white. This attracts attention because it is so placed that, by bringing the eye nearly to the level of the water, and looking along the surface, a reflection of the vaulting and the windows

FROM THE TRIFORIUM OF THE NORTH TRANSEPT.

may be seen. It is often covered with a board, which can be easily removed. The pulpit is under the second arch counting from the crossing on the north side, and opposite to it are desks occupied by the choir during the delivery of the sermon.

The Renaissance organ gallery is supported by classical columns. The organ was placed on it by the grand prior Guillaume Coterel in 1630. Above it may be seen the great modern rose of the west window. Underneath each of the windows of the aisles, except the fifth on each side, statues in plaster stand against the walls; all these are modern work. In the fifth bay on each side there are doorways, the one on the south being an entrance from the outside, that on the north leading into the long low building that skirts the base of the wall on the outside, as mentioned in the last chapter. This building has eight bays in all; the seven westernmost are used by the choir boys, and the one at the east is fitted up for the use of the curé. From this there is a passage leading through a most beautiful doorway into a fourteenth century chapel on the west side of the north transept.

In the priest's chamber are some of the treasures of the abbey, an eleventh century crozier, and a fourteenth century chair with a carving of a monk and the devil on it. The north end of the transept is fitted as a chapel, as will be seen in the illustration on p. 92. The corresponding end of the south transept opens into the Portail des Marmosets. It will be noticed that all round the church, above the arches of the arcading which divides the aisles from the nave and choir, a narrow passage runs behind a stone screen; this is the triforium, and it is lighted by a series of windows; above this tier, again, are the windows of the clerestory. The ends of the transepts are occupied by the celebrated rose windows aleady mentioned; that on the south is Alexander Berneval's; that on the north, according to tradition, was designed by one of his pupils whom he killed in a fit of jealousy. From the triforium on the opposite side the whole circles of these windows are not seen, as a pointed arch a few feet in front of them interrupts the view of the upper part of the circles.

From the chapel in the north transept a door leads into the interior of the **Tour aux Clercs.** This is at the present time empty, or only used as a receptacle for odds and ends.

Round **the choir** is a series of eleven chapels; the three easternmost on each side are rectangular, the others are formed of five sides of octagons. They contain altars, tapestry,

THE CHOIR.

and paintings. In the first chapel on the north side is the font, in the second the tomb of Berneval; three of the five faces of the fourth chapel each contain a two-light window. The vaulting of all these chapels is very beautiful. In the fifth chapel there are blocked-up windows in the first and fifth face, and glazed three-light windows in the other three. In the one on the left may be seen the so-called execution of Berneval. The sixth is the Lady Chapel, and is larger than any of the others. On either side is a wall running east and west, with the tracery of a blind window to the west and a three-light window to the east, then three sides of an octagon form the apsidal ending of the chapel; each contains a three-light window. The south side of the chevet corresponds exactly to the north. Beyond the octagonal chapels are three rectangular ones; from the central one of these a door leads into the rectangular building mentioned in the last chapter.[1]

The choir itself is divided from the aisles and ambulatory by an iron screen, with rich wrought-iron doors of the time of Louis XIV., the character of which will be seen from the illustration on p. 98, which represents the one on the south side of the choir; a corresponding one stands on the north side. Passing through one of these we gain admission to the choir and sanctuary. The three arches of the arcading that stand behind the altar are stilted, as may be seen from the illustration on p. 96; through these the windows of the Lady Chapel with their light geometrical tracery may be seen. There are two rows of stalls on either side of the choir, but these are not furnished with canopies.

At one time the choir was separated from the nave by a Gothic screen erected in 1462 by order of Cardinal Estouteville, who at that time was Abbot of St. Ouen. This was mutilated by the Protestants in 1562, repaired in 1655, and finally destroyed in 1791. The Protestant rioters at the same time that they damaged the screen destroyed the tomb of the abbot Marc d'Argent, the founder of the abbey, who died in January, 1339. He had, during his lifetime, prepared his

---

[1] On the occasion of the writer's visit, when he was taking the photographs from which the illustrations are reproduced, a couple came to the church to be married. The ecclesiastical part of the ceremony, which occupied but a short time, was performed in the westernmost of the three chapels on the south side, and then the wedding party proceeded in a body through the second chapel into the rectangular building, where, with much laughter and merriment, the legal formalities necessary to complete the marriage were gone through.

98   THE ABBEY CHURCH OF ST. OUEN.

last resting-place in the Lady Chapel. In this same chapel were buried Nicholas, the fourth abbot and founder of the

IRON DOORS OF CHOIR.

eleventh century church, who died February 26th, 1092, and Talbot, who perished during the English war in 1438.

ST. MACLOU.

ORGAN STAIRCASE.

ST. MACLOU.

CHAPTER I.

HISTORY OF THE BUILDING.

THE church of St. Maclou, inferior though it is in size to its neighbours, Notre Dame and St. Ouen, is a perfect gem, and is especially interesting to the English student of architecture, as it is a perfect specimen of that style of which no examples can be found on this side of the Channel—the Flamboyant, though here and there we may see, especially in Scotland, a window whose tracery has some trace of Flamboyant feeling.

Up to the fourteenth century, architecture ran much the same general course in Northern France that it did in England. The Romanesque of the eleventh and twelfth centuries, or, as we generally call it, the Norman, passed through a transitional period into the Early Pointed or Lancet style which flourished during the first half of the thirteenth century, developing then into what we call the Decorated style, which reached its perfection in the early part of the fourteenth century. There were, however, some characteristic differences between English and French architecture even in those days. English builders were satisfied in many cases to retain and modify the earlier buildings; while the aspiring French architect who set his heart on lofty vaults of stone, entirely swept away the old buildings, so that in Normandy far less architecture of the "Norman" style remains than in England. In the fourteenth century, however, a parting of ways took place: the Englishman set his heart on straight lines, the Frenchman continued to delight in curves, so that by the end of the fifteenth century there was little in common between English and French buildings, though architecture both in England and France was far inferior to what it had been in the glorious days of the second half of the thirteenth and first half of the fourteenth century. The Perpendicular style in England was a fresh departure in architecture, whereas the Flamboyant grew naturally out of the style prevalent in the fourteenth century. The fatal change in feeling which was to be the ruin of Gothic took place when line, as Mr. Ruskin tells us, took the place of mass as the element of decoration. And this love for flowing lines in France increased to a most extravagant extent, and many of the Flamboyant churches have the appearance of overdressed women as compared with the soberer grace of those built in earlier times.

Yet it cannot be denied that the Flamboyant style has a beauty, especially when its decoration is not carried to excess, and some there are who prefer even the exuberance of late Flamboyant to the frigid formality and poverty of design to be

WEST FRONT OF ST. MACLOU.

met with in much of the contemporary work in England. It would be hard to find an English church built at the same time as St. Maclou (which was commenced in 1436 and finished about the end of the same century) that can match it. Perhaps the most important building of this period in England is the Chapel of King's College, Cambridge. Where in that well known building can one find anything to match the life and terrible earnestness of the sculpture on the tympanum over the west door of St. Maclou? The English Perpendicular and the French Flamboyant builders were each alike over-profuse in use of ornament; both extinguished the second of the "Seven Lamps" of architecture, that of Truth; both delighted in showing their own cleverness, but the Frenchman possessed an exuberant fancy to which he gave full rein. His English contemporary was a matter-of-fact workman who took care to get as much ornamentation at as small an expenditure of brain-power and money as he could. He tolerated the repetition of ornament rather than take the trouble to invent something fresh. The Flamboyant and Perpendicular styles each died out in their respective homes when the revival of learning brought to light the masterpieces of Greek and Latin literature, and men began to think since the plays of Sophocles and the odes of Horace surpassed anything that they had been accustomed to read in their own languages, that therefore the buildings that adorned Periclean Athens and Imperial Rome must of necessity excel those which mediæval builders had raised in their own lands; hence an imitation of classical forms became common and the love for Gothic passed away. But Gothic architecture had already passed the period of its greatest strength and lay a-dying, but like the dying dolphin it showed, in France at anyrate, some beauties ere it finally passed away that it had never shown before, and some of these we meet with in the glorious church of St. Maclou.

We know but little of the saint to whom this church is dedicated. The first syllable of his name points to Scotch descent. It is said that he fled from his native land to Brittany, and became the Bishop of Aleth, a small town near the modern St. Malo, where may still be seen the ruins of a cathedral said to have been originally founded by him in the sixth century. The date of his death is said to be 561. A chapel was built and dedicated to him in the tenth century outside the then existing walls of Rouen. This was twice burnt, namely, in 1203 and 1211, and twice rebuilt; and owing to the extension of the city it became a parish church within its walls before the end of the thirteenth century. It was, however, in course of time found to be too small for the worshippers that wished to use it; so in 1432 it was resolved to take measures for entirely rebuilding it on a larger scale. An appeal was made to Archbishop Hugues of Rouen to aid in the work. Indulgences were granted to those who contributed to the cost of the building. In 1436 Pierre Robin furnished plans for the new church, for which work he was paid 43 livres, and the building was forthwith commenced. We first find Oudin de Mantes, and in 1446 Simon-le-Noir, directing the work, and in 1470 the name of Ambroise Harel is found; and ten years later Jacques le Roux, whom we have previously mentioned as working at Notre Dame, completed the body of the church. In 1520 a lead-covered spire was added, and a peal of six bells was hung in 1529. The celebrated doors were begun in 1527 and finished in 1560. Some of the carving is attributed to Jean Goujon, who was born in 1520, and worked both here and at Notre Dame in 1540 or 1541, and was killed while working at the Louvre in Paris at the time of the massacre of St. Bartholomew, 1572.

In 1705 great damage was done to the spire by a storm; and thirty years later, as it was considered unsafe, a considerable part of it was taken down. The complete destruction of it, however, was reserved for the time of the French Revolution, when the remaining lead was cast into bullets and the metal of the bells was converted into cannon. A new peal of five bells was provided in 1827, which were re-hung when the present lofty spire was completed in 1868.

The delicate stone tracery over the west portals has suffered from time to time from the effects of wind. At the beginning of 1900 the apex of the gable over the central door was blown down. Scaffolding was soon erected, and masons were at work repairing the damage when the writer visited the church at the beginning of May 1900. But during the afternoon of Sunday, May 6th, shortly after the service was over, a thunderstorm broke upon the city accompanied by a terrible whirlwind, and another massive pinnacle was torn down from the western façade and was shattered on the steps before the entrance.

Storms on many occasions have done damage to the churches of Rouen, and if they often have the violence of the storm of May 6th, 1900, one can easily understand how the lace-like tracery which decorates the western parts, standing free from the walls behind it, has been unable to resist the force of the wind, increased in power by rushing through the narrow streets of the city.

One more historical note must be given before passing on to the examination of the exterior of the building, namely, that the church was dedicated by Cardinal Georges d'Amboise II., Archbishop of Rouen, in 1521, when one Arthur Fillon was vicar of the parish. St. Maclou, it may be here observed, is now, as it has always been, a parish church pure and simple; and has never had any connection with any monastic body.

CHAPTER II.

THE EXTERIOR.

The part of the church to which most attention will naturally be directed is the splendid western front. Good general views of the church cannot be obtained. It is closely beset by houses; a narrow street, a continuation of the Rue St. Romain, opens opposite the west front; another narrow street, the Rue Martainville, runs along its north side, and a still narrower and more squalid street skirts it on the south. Workshops stand close to the south side, and only a glimpse of the east end with its flying buttresses can be got, for some buildings of recent date in classical style, apparently used for some parochial purposes, prevent the whole of the east end from being seen. The plan of the west front is peculiar: the church has, in fact, two apsidal endings, one at the east and one at the west. In the western façade we note first the wide central doorway under its arched porch, over which rises a lofty gable with Flamboyant tracery, partially supported by an open-work arcading which runs round the whole west end and is attached to the pinnacles, which rise between the five arches of the front. On either side of the main doorway are two side doors under similar but narrower porches, and again on either side of that still narrower arches or porticoes, gabled like the others, but without any doorways beneath them. Above the central doorway, behind its gable, is the fine western rose window, surmounted by a gable of its own. The whole west front is one bewildering mass of gables, pinnacles, crockets, gargoyles, statues, and pierced parapets, which it would take pages to describe in detail; so no attempt at description will be made; the reader is only asked to carefully examine the illustration on p. 102.

THE EXTERIOR. 107

In describing the tympanum over the west central doorway

TYMPANUM OF WEST DOOR.

Mr. Ruskin's eloquent words from *The Seven Lamps of Archi-*

tecture, page 167, must be quoted. "The subject of the tympanum bas-relief is the Last Judgment, and the sculpture on the inferno side is carried out with a degree of power whose fearful grotesqueness I can only describe as a mingling of the minds of Orcagna and Hogarth. The demons are perhaps more awful than Orcagna's; and in some of the expressions of debased humanity in its utmost despair the English painter is at least equalled. Not less wild is the imagination which gives fury and fear even to the placing of the figures. An evil angel poised on the wing drives the condemned troops from before the judgment-seat; with his left hand he drags behind him a cloud, which he is spreading like a winding-sheet over them all; but they are urged by him so furiously, that they are driven not merely to the extreme limit of that scene, which the sculptor confined elsewhere within the tympanum, but out of the tympanum and *into the niches* of the arch, while the flames that follow them, bent by the blast as it seems of the angel's wings, rush into the niches also, and burst up through their tracery, the three lowest niches being represented as all on fire, while, instead of their usual vaulted and ribbed ceiling, there is a demon in the roof of each, with his wings folded over it, grinning down out of the black shadow."

If the tympanum is worthy of attention, so are the doors below. The legend concerning them is that they were carved by St. Michael the archangel, and were brought from Rome to Rouen by the devil in a single night; though for what reason he gave himself the trouble thus to benefit Rouen at the expense of Rome the legend fails to tell. With a nearer approach to the truth they have been attributed to Jean Goujon, but they could not well have been entirely the work of his own chisel. In the great central doorway there are two doors opening right and left; in the doorway to the left is a single door, and another on the north side of the church opens into the Rue Martainville. Each door is divided into two parts; in the lower half there is a small door or wicket sufficiently large to admit one person at a time when the large doors are closed. On one side of the great central door one may see prophets and Jewish priests, on the other the evangelists and Christian priests; the subject carved on the circular medallion set in a square panel;

on the left is the Circumcision, and that on the corresponding right hand medallion is the baptism of Christ by John.

PART OF WEST DOOR.

The former panel is supported by St. Gregory, St. Jerome, St. Augustine, and St. Ambrose, the latter by the four evangelists. On the sides we see Enoch, Elijah, Moses, and Gideon; on the sides of the lower part of the door are carved allegorical figures representing Peace, Justice, Faith, and Charity. At the head of the door is a representation of the Father before and after the creation.

The door of the left hand portal is carved within and without with subjects taken from the Parable of the Good Shepherd. Within we see on one side the Good Shepherd defending his flock; on the other the hireling abandoning his sheep to the wolf. On the outside on the medallion Christ is represented as the Good Shepherd, standing in front of a sheepfold from which robbers are trying to steal the sheep. He addresses four men, of whom one is a pope, one a king, and one a theologian; four figures, which it is difficult to identify, support this panel, and behind them stand representations of Winter, Spring, and Summer. Above, the hand of Jehovah may be seen issuing from a cloud; on the sides of the door are carved Melchizedek and Aaron, Peter and Paul. The door on the south side of the great portal is not carved. The doors on the north side of the church are carved on both sides: on the inner is represented the story of the Prodigal Son, on the outer are subjects celebrating the history of the Virgin, whose statue stands on a pillar in the middle of the doorway. On the doors are two medallions, one representing the ark of the covenant, the other the death of St. Mary, round whose bed stand the apostles. Above may be seen, on the one hand, Jehovah at the burning bush, on the other God the Son. Each of the medallions, set in square panels, is supported by four saints. The beautiful doors suffered from the violence of the Protestants in 1562, and again from the Revolutionary mob in 1793. When the west front and the doors and the spire have been seen, there is nothing else that calls for notice in the exterior of the church, save possibly a much dilapidated fountain in constant use for the drawing of water at the north-west corner of the church.

VIEW FROM THE WEST.

CHAPTER III.

THE INTERIOR.

ON entering the church of St. Maclou, one cannot fail to be struck by its great height in proportion to its length, for the whole length is but 180 feet, and the vaulting of the nave is 75 feet from the floor, and as the lower stage of the central tower forms a lantern each face of which is lit by two three-light windows, we can look up to a height of no less than 128 feet. Next we shall probably regret that better taste has not prevailed in the decoration of the eastern arm of the church. The old Gothic screen, which formerly separated the choir from the crossing, was removed in 1727, and in its place was put up a scrolled arch of wood surmounted by a crucifix standing between two angels. Over the high altar is a carving of the resurrection, in which heavy beams of gilded wood are supposed to represent sun rays and heavy masses of wood have to be taken as symbolical of clouds. The shafts of the pillars between the sanctuary and the ambulatory have been cased in wood; all this is in the worst possible taste. The pulpit, a rather heavy-looking erection with a sounding-board above it, was set up in 1621, and stands on the south side of the nave close to the south-west pillar that supports the tower; on its panels are carved scenes from the Parable of the Sower. There are three rose windows: one on the west front and one at each end of the transept; the piers of the nave arcading are entirely without capitals; above this arcading is a dark triforium, and above this again the clerestory. There are only three bays to the nave, but opposite to each of these, on either side beyond the aisles, is a side chapel. Next comes the transept, which has no aisles; beyond this the choir of two bays, on either side, opposite to each of which is a chapel outside the aisle; then four more bays in the apsidal ending, and four radiating chapels, each composed of five sides of an octagon. From the fact of there being an even number of chapels, there is no chapel stretching out to the east of the high altar; and for the same reason, there is a pillar behind the altar, and also the division between the two eastern windows of the clerestory appears in the centre.

The chief gem of the interior is the staircase leading to the organ. The organ loft is to be found in its usual place, over the western portal and beneath the western rose. It is supported by two classical columns of black marble, one on either side of the central doorway. The staircase is of carved stone, and stands on the south side. It bears some resemblance to the winding staircase which leads up to the organ in the north aisle of Ely Cathedral; in fact, the Ely staircase is said to be an imitation of that at St. Maclou. The nature of the beautiful open-work tracery of this will be easily seen on examining the illustration on p. 100. It was built in the years 1518–1519, by one Pierre Gringoire, master-mason of Rouen, who for his work received the sum of 205 livres.

Aître S. Maclou.

No visitor to St. Maclou should leave the neighbourhood without seeing the Aître. Yet many never hear of it, and if they do not, are little likely to find it by chance; for though it lies close at hand it is entered by a passage under an archway which apparently leads nowhere. We must pass along the Rue Martainville, that runs along the north side of the church, keeping a good look-out on the left hand or north side of the street. Before long we shall see an opening, and at the upper end of the passage into which this leads, written across one of the beams of a half timber house, we shall discern the words "Cloître S. Maclou." We must go up this passage under the beam, and turn through a little gate on the right hand, and shall then find ourselves in a square surrounded on every side by low two-storied buildings, with dormer windows in the roofs above. But we see at once that they are no ordinary dwelling-houses. The ground floor consists of a row of windows divided by wooden pillars carved indeed, though what the subjects are it is hard to tell, so worn away are they; but above the windows runs a double line of frieze carved in oak, and on these we can easily make out the carvings to be ghastly emblems of the sexton's business—

AÎTRE S. MACLOU.

mattocks, spades, skulls, crossbones, and coffin lids; above the frieze we see another row of windows beneath the overhanging eaves; to this upper story covered staircases at the corners of the square lead up. Probably among those signs of mortality we may find children at play or taking exercise; in one part girls under the watchful eye of sisters in garb of grey, with those large white starched caps that it is such a marvel they can keep so stiff and spotless, and in another boys under the charge of a priest habited in a cassock. For these galleries round the old cemetery have been converted into charity schools. The rectangular enclosure measures some 150 feet in length by about 100 feet in breadth, and is divided into two parts by walls and railings, one for the boys and the other for the girls; the former occupy the south and east sides, the latter the two other sides. Beneath the feet of these playing children lie the remains of countless hosts of nameless dead; for this was one of the old burying-grounds of the city in mediæval times, and was especially used as the last resting-place of the victims of that terrible plague from which mediæval Europe suffered so much over and over again. We are apt to fancy that the Great Plague of London was an isolated visitation, but it was not so; in the fourteenth century, the plague or the "Black Death," as it was called, devastated England, sweeping away, some say a third, some say a half or even more of the population of our country, so that much of the land remained untilled for lack of labourers, and the survivors were able to demand higher wages, and to raise themselves from the condition of serfdom that they had practically endured before, while at the same time much of the land fell into the hands of the Church. And ever and again there were outbreaks of plague in various parts of England, for this frightful malady found a fitting soil wherein to flourish in the filthy streets of overcrowded towns and cities and the miserable abodes of the poor. And not only England suffered, but other countries of Europe also. And among other cities Rouen suffered. The visitor to the Rouen of to-day, as he walks along the wide boulevards with their rows of shady trees, or along the main thoroughfares such as the Rue Jeanne d'Arc, or rests in the well-kept public gardens, may think the city a clean, well-ordered place; but let him go in search of the picturesque into the back streets and byways, where the remains of old Rouen still linger, and he will change his mind. He will find narrow alleys with projecting houses, open gutters, noisome odours pervading the air, and may form some idea of what Rouen was in the days when these splendid fabrics which have been described in this book were being raised.

It was an unhealthy place to dwell in; its eighty cemeteries were crowded with dead, the air was constantly infected with pestilence; and from the thirteenth century onwards it was ravaged by disease. In 1348 the Black Death claimed no less than 100,000 victims in this city alone. It was at this time that the cemetery of St. Maclou was formed. In this graveyard stood an altar to St. Michael, the saint of the dead, and the conductor of souls to Paradise. And the brotherhood of St. Michael devoted itself to the carrying of dead bodies to their graves. The graveyard, on more than one occasion, had to be enlarged, for the space was too narrow for the dead who sought interment here. However, by 1526, the circumscribing galleries on the east, south, and west ends that we see to-day had been built; the other was not finished for more than a hundred years after. We have all read of the strange condition of life in plague-stricken cities, when death is carrying off men, women, and children by hundreds. We hear how those who have as yet escaped give way to revelry and license. And so it was at Rouen. In the fourteenth century we hear of the hideous "Danse Macabre," when the people were seized with mad frenzy and leapt and danced in wild hysterical convulsions in the open street, in the church, and in the burying-ground. This state of mind found its expressions in many a mediæval carving of the Devil and his angels carrying off souls to endless flame; but in course of time the place of the Devil was taken by Death, and we have in various places paintings, carvings, and engravings of the Dance of Death in which a grisly skeleton is represented dancing with men and women of every degree—the king, the bishop, the noble and the peasant, the high-born lady and the serving maid, old and young alike. And the carvings that we can hardly make out on the pillars of the Aître St. Maclou, when they were fresh from the chisel, might have been seen to be representations of this grim idea. It was some consolation to the poor man who had to die that the wealthy noble or merchant whose good things he had envied, and the tyrant who had oppressed him, would be overtaken at last by the same fate as that in store for himself. So round the cemetery in which the poor man found his last resting-place, with no stone or post, no line of inscription to keep his memory alive, death was represented hurrying off the great of this world to the inevitable end. For this

"Aître" was especially the graveyard of the poor, though some of the wealthier citizens were buried within the galleries that surround the central space. In course of time the city became more healthy; and it is recorded of the great Georges d'Amboise I. that not only was he full of kindness to the victims of the plague, but that he did his best to render the city a more wholesome place to dwell in. Not only did he enrich the cathedral church and other ecclesiastical buildings, but also set on foot sanitary reforms and improved the water-supply of the city. An enactment of 1520 may be here mentioned, namely, one forbidding the building of houses with overhanging fronts, a most insanitary practice, since it made the streets, often narrow enough at the bottom, still narrower where the upper stories almost met, and so prevented the free circulation of air and the admission of sunlight—the best disinfectants, and the most potent enemies of disease in all the world.

APPENDIX I.

Dimensions of the Three Churches.

Notre Dame.

	Ft.
Total length,	450
Width across Transepts,	177
Width across Nave and Aisles,	105
Width across Western Façade,	190
Height of Nave Vault,	92
Length of Choir,	118
Width of Choir,	39
Length of Lady Chapel,	75
Width of Lady Chapel,	26
Height of Lady Chapel,	62
Height of Central Spire,	480
Height of Central Lantern,	174
Height of Butter Tower,	252
Height of St. Romain's Tower,	246

St. Ouen.

	Ft.
Total length,	450
Width across the Transepts,	150
Width across Nave and Aisles,	84
Width across Nave,	34
Height of Vault,	100
Length of Choir,	100
Width of Choir with Chapels,	135
Length of Lady Chapel,	36
Height of Central Tower,	265

St. Maclou.

	Ft.
Total Length,	180
Width,	80
Height of Vault,	75
Height of Lantern,	128
Height of Spire,	289

APPENDIX II.

The Minor Churches of Rouen.

WERE it not that the three churches already described surpass in size and beauty all the rest to so great an extent, there would be several others demanding a longer notice than the remaining space at the writer's disposal permits him to give them; still, as the visitor to Rouen may be glad not to omit anything worth study from not knowing of its existence, a few words shall here be said.

In the extreme north-west of the city stands **St. Gervais,** a curiosity in its way, for it is a nineteenth century church built in twelfth century style, but the one ancient part of it, namely, the crypt beneath the floor of the present chancel, is the oldest Christian building in Rouen, and one of the oldest in Northern Europe. It can only be seen by artificial light, and the candle carried by the custodian of the church does little more than make darkness visible; however, after one's eyes have become accustomed to the gloom, the tombs of St. Mellon and St. Avitiar may be made out on the north and south sides respectively, and also the stone altar at the east end. It is a tiny church, with nave covered with a barrel roof and an eastern apse, and was built by St. Victrice in the early part of the fifth century. It was in a monastery that formerly existed here that William the Conqueror died.

Right across the city to the extreme south-east stands the next church to which attention must be directed, namely, **St. Paul's.** This, like St. Gervais, is a modern church built in twelfth century style, and its only interest lies in the apse, all that remains of an older church which was destroyed when the existing St. Paul's was built, and which is now used as a vestry. The axis of the old church pointed to that point on the horizon from which the sun rises in summer, the axis of the new to that point from which it rises in winter, probably on the Feast of the Conversion of St. Paul; hence the axis of the old apse is roughly at right angles to that of the modern church. This ancient fragment once formed part of the church, connected with a convent in which dwelt about half a dozen nuns; this was suppressed in 1650 and the nuns sent to Montivilliers. The church, however, was always parochial as well as conventual. Legend attributes the foundation of this building to St. Romain, but the existing Norman apse is much later, probably eleventh century. The corbels are carved into heads of bearded figures, and probably represent foreigners with whom the Normans came into conflict; for the Norman warriors, as we all have heard, were close shaven at the time when William landed in England, and were consequently taken by the English for ecclesiastics. The nave of the church, which was destroyed when the new one was built (1827-1829), dated from the seventeenth century only.

These two churches have been mentioned first on account of their antiquity, so much greater than that of any others yet to be described. Next to St. Maclou in point of importance comes **St. Vincent.** The church, as we see it now, dates chiefly from the sixteenth century; the tower is still later. The western porch is the chief attraction on the outside, and among the treasures of its interior are some sixteenth century tapestry and its painted windows. One of these represents a miracle performed by St. Antoine of Padua. He was preaching at Toulouse, and the heretics refused to believe unless the saint's mule, after having been kept without food for several days, when placed between the sacred Host and a measure of barley, would turn aside from the corn to adore the Host. This the mule duly did, and the heretics embraced the Christian faith.

St. Patrice, dedicated to the Irish saint, is chiefly noted for its painted glass, most of it due to the sixteenth century.

St. Laurent has fallen upon evil days. The lower stages of its beautiful tower are occupied as residences, and the body of the church has been converted into shops and furniture warehouses. The old church of St. Laurent perished in the fire of 1248, which destroyed its near neighbour St. Goddard and also the abbey church of St. Ouen. The rebuilding was begun in the fourteenth century; the tower, finished in 1501, fell in 1520 and was then rebuilt; some parts again fell in 1677, but it was repaired.

St. Goddard stands near St. Laurent's, on the site of an earlier chapel dedicated to the Virgin, which, when the Archbishop St. Goddard was buried within its walls, took his name. The existing church dates from the fifteenth and sixteenth centuries. In 1801 some of its painted windows were given to the churches of St. Ouen and St. Patrice. Some of the former stored in the Tour aux Clercs were broken, but two were replaced in St. Goddard's in 1806, when the church once more became parochial. One of these represents the Gargouille legend, and is interesting in that it shows that St. Romain had a second string to his bow in the shape of a second condemned prisoner to be used as bait for the monster if the first should fail to entice her from her lair. These two windows are sixteenth century work.

The church of **St. Nicaise** is dedicated to another monster-destroying saint, who came from Athens, was consecrated as Bishop of Rouen by the Pope Clement, Peter's immediate successor, and brought Christianity to Northern Gaul. St. Ouen obtained some of the relics of this saint and founded a chapel in his honour, which in course of time, being embraced by the extended boundaries of the city, became a parish church. In the sixteenth century the previously existing church was swept away and the choirs of a new one erected; the nave has never been completed.

St. Vivien has nothing very noteworthy about it beyond its fine square tower and the octagonal spire that rises from it, well seen from the Place St. Vivien.

St. Romain, once the chapel of the Carmelites, is a church in the Renaissance style 1676–1730, and is chiefly interesting from the fact that it contains some glass which formerly adorned the windows of other churches which were suppressed, and the tomb of St. Romain, which once stood in the crypt of St. Goddard, where the body of the saint rested, until the Huguenot rioters disturbed it in 1582 and scattered his dust to the winds. The tomb was removed to the church of St. Romain in 1802, and over it the high altar was erected.

None of the other churches deserve any special notice.

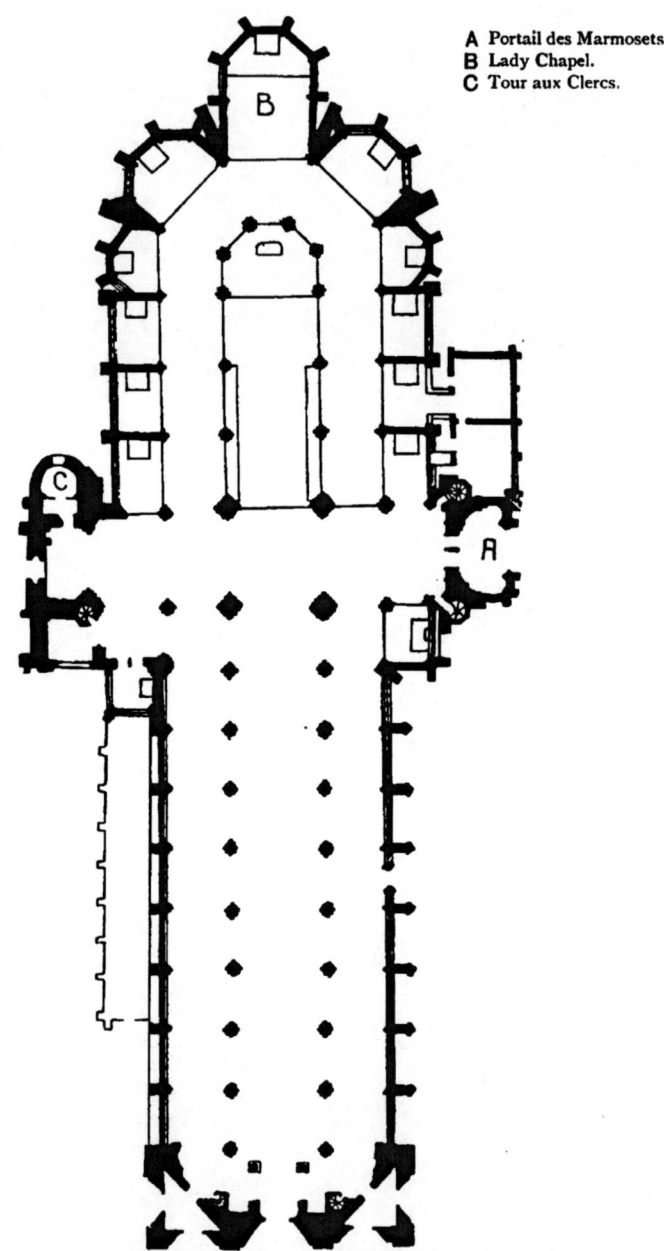

GROUND PLAN OF S. OUEN.

A Portail des Marmosets.
B Lady Chapel.
C Tour aux Clercs.

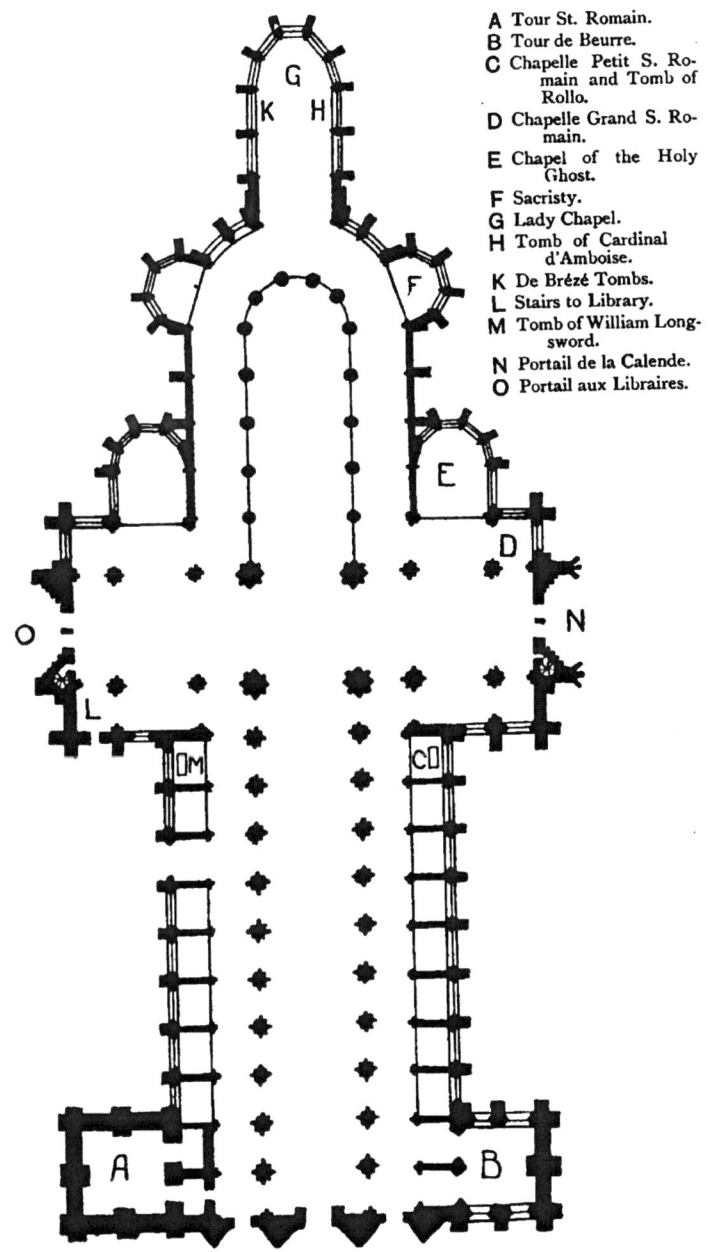

GROUND PLAN OF ROUEN CATHEDRAL.

A Tour St. Romain.
B Tour de Beurre.
C Chapelle Petit S. Romain and Tomb of Rollo.
D Chapelle Grand S. Romain.
E Chapel of the Holy Ghost.
F Sacristy.
G Lady Chapel.
H Tomb of Cardinal d'Amboise.
K De Brézé Tombs.
L Stairs to Library.
M Tomb of William Longsword.
N Portail de la Calende.
O Portail aux Libraires.

PRINTED BY
NEILL AND COMPANY, LIMITED
BELLEVUE, EDINBURGH

Bell's Cathedral Series.

Profusely Illustrated. Cloth, crown 8vo, **1s. 6d.** *each.*

NOW READY.

CANTERBURY. By Hartley Withers. 3rd Edition, revised.
CARLISLE. By C. K. Eley.
CHESTER. By Charles Hiatt. 2nd Edition, revised.
DURHAM. By J. E. Bygate, A.R.C.A. 2nd Edition.
EXETER. By Percy Addleshaw, B.A. 2nd Edition.
GLOUCESTER. By H. J. L. J. Massé, M.A. 2nd Edition.
HEREFORD. By A. Hugh Fisher, A.R.E.
LICHFIELD. By A. B. Clifton. 2nd Edition, revised.
LINCOLN. By A. F. Kendrick, B.A. 2nd Edition, revised.
NORWICH. By C. H. B. Quennell. 2nd Edition.
OXFORD. By Rev. Percy Dearmer, M.A. 2nd Edition, revised.
PETERBOROUGH. By Rev. W. D. Sweeting, M.A. 2nd Edition.
ROCHESTER. By G. H. Palmer, B.A. 2nd Edition.
ST. PAUL'S. By Rev. Arthur Dimock, M.A. 2nd Edition.
SALISBURY. By Gleeson White. 2nd Edition, revised.
SOUTHWELL. By Rev. Arthur Dimock, M.A.
WELLS. By Rev. Percy Dearmer, M.A. 2nd Edition, revised.
WINCHESTER. By P. W. Sergeant. 2nd Edition, revised.
YORK. By A. Clutton Brock. 2nd Edition, revised.

Preparing.

ST. DAVID'S. By Philip Robson, A.R.I.B.A.
CHICHESTER. By H. C. Corlette, A.R.I.B.A.
WORCESTER. By E. F. Strange.
RIPON. By Cecil Hallet, B.A.
ELY. By Rev. W. D. Sweeting, M.A.
ST. ALBANS. By Rev. W. D. Sweeting, M.A.
BRISTOL. By H. J. L. J. Massé, M.A.
ST. ASAPH'S and BANGOR. By P. B. Ironside Bax.
GLASGOW. By P. Macgregor Chalmers, I.A., F.S.A. (Scot).

Uniform with above Series.

ST. MARTIN'S CHURCH, CANTERBURY. By Rev. Canon Routledge, M.A., F.S.A. 24 Illustrations.
BEVERLEY MINSTER. By Charles Hiatt. 47 Illustrations.
WIMBORNE MINSTER AND CHRISTCHURCH PRIORY. By Rev. T. Perkins, M.A., F.R.A.S. 65 Illustrations.
TEWKESBURY ABBEY AND DEERHURST PRIORY. By H. J. L. J. Massé, M.A. 44 Illustrations.
WESTMINSTER ABBEY. By Charles Hiatt. [*Preparing.*

Bell's Handbooks to Continental Churches.

Profusely Illustrated. Crown 8vo, cloth, **2s. 6d.** *each.*

CHARTRES: The Cathedral and Other Churches. By H. J. L. J. Massé, M.A. [*Ready.*
ROUEN: The Cathedral and Other Churches. By the Rev. T. Perkins, M.A. [*In the Press.*
PARIS (NOTRE-DAME). By Charles Hiatt. [*Preparing.*

LONDON: GEORGE BELL AND SONS,
YORK STREET, COVENT GARDEN, W.C.

Opinions of the Press.

"For the purpose at which they aim they are admirably done, and there are few visitors to any of our noble shrines who will not enjoy their visit the better for being furnished with one of these delightful books, which can be slipped into the pocket and carried with ease, and is yet distinct and legible. . . . A volume such as that on Canterbury is exactly what we want, and on our next visit we hope to have it with us. It is thoroughly helpful, and the views of the fair city and its noble cathedral are beautiful. Both volumes, moreover, will serve more than a temporary purpose, and are trustworthy as well as delightful."—*Notes and Queries.*

"We have so frequently in these columns urged the want of cheap, well-illustrated, and well-written handbooks to our cathedrals, to take the place of the out-of-date publications of local booksellers, that we are glad to hear that they have been taken in hand by Messrs George Bell & Sons."—*St. James's Gazette.*

"The volumes are handy in size, moderate in price, well illustrated, and written in a scholarly spirit. The history of cathedral and city is intelligently set forth and accompanied by a descriptive survey of the building in all its detail. The illustrations are copious and well selected, and the series bids fair to become an indispensable companion to the cathedral tourist in England."—*Times.*

"They are nicely produced in good type, on good paper, and contain numerous illustrations, are well written, and very cheap. We should imagine architects and students of architecture will be sure to buy the series as they appear, for they contain in brief much valuable information." —*British Architect.*

"Bell's 'Cathedral Series,' so admirably edited, is more than a description of the various English cathedrals. It will be a valuable historical record, and a work of much service also to the architect. The illustrations are well selected, and in many cases not mere bald architectural drawings but reproductions of exquisite stone fancies, touched in their treatment by fancy and guided by art."—*Star.*

"Each of them contains exactly that amount of information which the intelligent visitor, who is not a specialist, will wish to have. The disposition of the various parts is judiciously proportioned, and the style is very readable. The illustrations supply a further important feature; they are both numerous and good. A series which cannot fail to be welcomed by all who are interested in the ecclesiastical buildings of England."— *Glasgow Herald.*

"Those who, either for purposes of professional study or for a cultured recreation, find it expedient to 'do' the English cathedrals will welcome the beginning of Bell's 'Cathedral Series.' This set of books is an attempt to consult, more closely, and in greater detail than the usual guide-books do, the needs of visitors to the cathedral towns. The series cannot but prove markedly successful. In each book a business-like description is given of the fabric of the church to which the volume relates, and an interesting history of the relative diocese. The books are plentifully illustrated, and are thus made attractive as well as instructive. They cannot but prove welcome to all classes of readers interested either in English Church history or in ecclesiastical architecture."—*Scotsman.*

"They have nothing in common with the almost invariably wretched local guides save portability, and their only competitors in the quality and quantity of their contents are very expensive and mostly rare works, each of a size that suggests a packing-case rather than a coat-pocket. The 'Cathedral Series' are important compilations concerning history, architecture, and biography, and quite popular enough for such as take any sincere interest in their subjects."—*Sketch.*

LONDON: GEORGE BELL AND SONS

CPSIA information can be obtained at www.ICGtesting.com
Printed in the USA
LVOW10*2212210316

480174LV00008B/53/P